Windows Phone 7.5: Building Location-aware Applications

Build your first Windows Phone application with Location and Maps

Zeeshan Chawdhary

[PACKT] enterprise
PUBLISHING
professional expertise distilled

BIRMINGHAM - MUMBAI

Windows Phone 7.5: Building Location-aware Applications

First published: July 2012

Production Reference: 1120712

Published by Packt Publishing Ltd.
Livery Place
35 Livery Street
Birmingham B3 2PB, UK.

ISBN 978-1-84968-724-9

www.packtpub.com

Cover Image by Mark Holland (m.j.g.holland@bham.ac.uk)

Credits

Author
Zeeshan Chawdhary

Reviewers
John Baird
Feyaerts David
I.T. Lackey

Acquisition Editor
Dilip Venkatesh

Lead Technical Editor
Arun Nadar

Technical Editor
Manmeet Singh Vasir

Copy Editor
Alfida Paiva

Project Coordinators
Kushal Bhardwaj
Michelle Quadros

Proofreaders
Chris Brown
Christopher Smith

Indexer
Rekha Nair

Production Coordinator
Aparna Bhagat

Cover Work
Aparna Bhagat

About the Author

Zeeshan Chawdhary has over six years of experience in the Web and Mobile space. With a career spanning from developing 3D mobile games at Indiagames Ltd to leading the location-based space at Wcities, Inc. as the Chief Technology Officer, Zeeshan has been able to learn quite a lot in the Mobile and Web domain and in a short space of time.

Among his key achievements is the pioneering use of the right mix of open source and proprietary software to create a technology stack based on clients' needs. He has developed location-based solutions for Nokia (with 5 million hits per year!) on a scalable cloud platform using Rackspace Cloud. He enjoys working with PHP, PostGIS, and PhoneGap. He has immense experience in making startups use location data effectively for their growth, from startups such as Foursquare to hotel industry bigwigs such as Marriott, from mobile giant Nokia to airline king American Airlines; he has worked with them all.

Zeeshan Chawdhary currently serves as the CTO of Wcities, Inc. where he is working on connected-car technologies. He can be reached at imzeeshanc@gmail.com.

Firstly, I am grateful to God, for he made me what I am. Coming to Earth, I would like to thank my parents, who have always been supportive of my love of books and computers. I would also like to thank my wife Sundus, who has been a great support while I wrote this book in the wee hours. I would also like to thank my brother and sister, for enduring me all these years.

About the Reviewers

John Baird is the founder of Xamlware, a professional consulting firm specializing in Silverlight and Windows Phone 7 development. John has 30 years of experience in designing, coding, and implementing software solutions.

John co-founded the Northern Delaware .Net Users Group, is heavily involved in the local .NET communities, and travels extensively, presenting to user groups, code camps, and special interest groups. John is also a four-time recipient of Microsoft's MVP award for Windows Phone 7.

Feyaerts David has worked on .NET technologies for more than three years. After completing a Bachelor's degree in Informatique and System, he worked as a Software Engineer at BizzDev (Belgium).

David works predominantly on C# and .NET, and was quickly promoted to a project leader. He works on multiple projects such as desktop applications (ERP), mobile applications (Windows Mobile and Windows Phone), ASP.NET websites, and so on.

To validate his expertise on .NET technologies, David is both a **Microsoft Certified Professional Developer (MCPD)** and **Microsoft Certified Technology Specialist (MCTS)** on Silverlight 4.

As a mobile developer for his employer he participates in development of an e-Health application for Windows Phone. He appreciates the Windows Phone platform as it is easy to use and provides new opportunities for design.

During this personal time, David also works independently as a developer for Windows Phone applications. At the time of writing, he was working on his ninth application.

Ian Lackey worked as a systems engineer for a St. Louis-based ISP from 1999 to 2002. At that time, he began developing web applications using ASP and migrated to ASP.NET shortly before the 2.0 release. Ian now works as a full-time developer for the Pediatrics department of Washington University's School of Medicine. He also runs a small business, DigitalSnap Inc. (`http://www.digitalsnap.net`), which primarily provides custom Silverlight software, LightSwitch applications, individual DotNetNuke modules (`http://www.itlackey.net`), as well as custom and commercial Windows Phone 7 applications.

Ian is currently involved in community-driven areas such as the OpenLight Group (`http://www.openlightgroup.net`), which manages open source projects including several DotNetNuke modules and many Silverlight-based applications. He has also co-authored a book with Michael Washington (*Building Websites with DotNetNuke 5, Michael Washington and Ian Lackey, Packt Publishing*), and was one of the reviewers for the book *Windows Phone 7 Data Cookbook, Ramesh Thalli, Packt Publishing*. Ian currently lives in a small town in Illinois, just east of St. Louis, with his wife Julie and two daughters, Britney and Brooklynn.

To my favorite ball player and my favorite dancer – Keep doing what you love, loving what you do, and simply be your beautiful self!

www.PacktPub.com

Support files, eBooks, discount offers and more

You might want to visit www.PacktPub.com for support files and downloads related to your book.

Did you know that Packt offers eBook versions of every book published, with PDF and ePub files available? You can upgrade to the eBook version at www.PacktPub.com and as a print book customer, you are entitled to a discount on the eBook copy. Get in touch with us at service@packtpub.com for more details.

At www.PacktPub.com, you can also read a collection of free technical articles, sign up for a range of free newsletters and receive exclusive discounts and offers on Packt books and eBooks.

http://PacktLib.PacktPub.com

Do you need instant solutions to your IT questions? PacktLib is Packt's online digital book library. Here, you can access, read and search across Packt's entire library of books.

Why Subscribe?

- Fully searchable across every book published by Packt
- Copy and paste, print and bookmark content
- On demand and accessible via web browser

Free Access for Packt account holders

If you have an account with Packt at www.PacktPub.com, you can use this to access PacktLib today and view nine entirely free books. Simply use your login credentials for immediate access.

Instant Updates on New Packt Books

Get notified! Find out when new books are published by following @PacktEnterprise on Twitter, or the *Packt Enterprise* Facebook page.

Table of Contents

Preface

Windows Phone 7.5: Building Location-aware Applications, introduces you to the exciting new world of Windows Phone 7.5. This book focuses on location-based applications, by introducing the readers to location-based services and the background thereof, coupled with practical examples for the Windows Phone location services. Another important discussion in the location context is maps, which is covered in great detail, including concepts such as geocoding and map directions.

This book will quickly teach you how to build Windows Phone 7.5 applications by leveraging location, maps, and third-party APIs. Two real-world applications are covered in depth: one using the excellent Events API from `Eventful.com`, and the other application, which focusses on location-aware news content powered by AOL's `Patch.com` News API.

What this book covers

Chapter 1, *The Location-based World*, explains location-based services, how they work, the important role of GPS in location-based services, and how Microsoft uses them in Windows Phone.

Chapter 2, *Using Location in Windows Phone 7.5*, starts with an introduction to the Windows Phone ecosystem and later on covers in-depth information on the Windows Phone Location Service and the Windows Phone location simulator.

Chapter 3, *Using Maps in your Windows Phone App*, introduces the reader to the world of Bing Maps; from working with a simple maps application to building a complex maps app with geocoding, directions, and local search.

Chapter 4, Events App – PacktEvents, covers building an events app that shows us nearby events, concerts, and gigs by artists by using the excellent `Eventful.com` API. The Windows Phone Panorama control is used to build this app.

Chapter 5, Location-aware News App – PacktNews, uses the Windows Phone Pivot control to build a hyperlocal news app—powered by AOL's Patch News API.

What you need for this book

To run the examples and the apps provided in the book, you will need a Windows PC with Windows 7 or higher and Microsoft Visual Studio 2010 Express for Windows Phone.

Some examples will need an API key from `Eventful.com` and `Patch.com`; the links are duly mentioned at the beginning of the chapters having such examples.

Who this book is for

If you are a developer who wants to develop apps for the Windows Phone 7.5 platform, but do not know where to begin, then this book is for you. Developers working on the Android and iPhone platform wishing to port their apps on the Windows Phone ecosystem will also find this book useful. The example code files and apps present in the book can also help a non-developer, such as a smart business or sales person, to quickly analyze and build new applications.

This book is also aimed at managers and architects in the news and entertainment industry, as two giants of this industry (`Eventful.com` and `Patch.com`) are mentioned extensively within the book.

Conventions

In this book, you will find a number of styles of text that distinguish between different kinds of information. Here are some examples of these styles, and an explanation of their meaning.

Code words in text are shown as follows: "The main class that handles Location Service is the `GeoCoordinateWatcher` class."

A block of code is set as follows:

```
latitudeText.Text=
locationManager.Position.Location.Latitude.ToString("0.000");
longitudeText.Text =
locationManager.Position.Location.Longitude.ToString("0.000");
```

When we wish to draw your attention to a particular part of a code block, the relevant lines or items are set in bold:

```
<Button Content="Start" Height="72"
    HorizontalAlignment="Left" Margin="0,35,0,0"
    Name="startButton" VerticalAlignment="Top" Width="160"
    Click="startButton_Click" />
```

New terms and **important words** are shown in bold. Words that you see on the screen, in menus or dialog boxes for example, appear in the text like this: "Open Visual Studio 2010 Express and create a new project by clicking on the **File | New Project** menu option.".

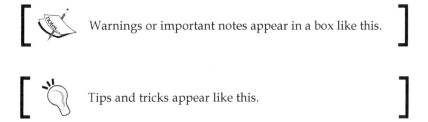

Warnings or important notes appear in a box like this.

Tips and tricks appear like this.

Reader feedback

Feedback from our readers is always welcome. Let us know what you think about this book—what you liked or may have disliked. Reader feedback is important for us to develop titles that you really get the most out of.

To send us general feedback, simply send an e-mail to feedback@packtpub.com, and mention the book title through the subject of your message.

If there is a topic that you have expertise in and you are interested in either writing or contributing to a book, see our author guide on www.packtpub.com/authors.

Customer support

Now that you are the proud owner of a Packt book, we have a number of things to help you to get the most from your purchase.

Downloading the example code

You can download the example code files for all Packt books you have purchased from your account at http://www.packtpub.com. If you purchased this book elsewhere, you can visit http://www.packtpub.com/support and register to have the files e-mailed directly to you.

Errata

Although we have taken every care to ensure the accuracy of our content, mistakes do happen. If you find a mistake in one of our books—maybe a mistake in the text or the code—we would be grateful if you would report this to us. By doing so, you can save other readers from frustration and help us improve subsequent versions of this book. If you find any errata, please report them by visiting http://www.packtpub.com/support, selecting your book, clicking on the **errata submission form** link, and entering the details of your errata. Once your errata are verified, your submission will be accepted and the errata will be uploaded to our website, or added to any list of existing errata, under the Errata section of that title.

Piracy

Piracy of copyright material on the Internet is an ongoing problem across all media. At Packt, we take the protection of our copyright and licenses very seriously. If you come across any illegal copies of our works, in any form, on the Internet, please provide us with the location address or website name immediately so that we can pursue a remedy.

Please contact us at copyright@packtpub.com with a link to the suspected pirated material.

We appreciate your help in protecting our authors, and our ability to bring you valuable content.

Questions

You can contact us at questions@packtpub.com if you are having a problem with any aspect of the book, and we will do our best to address it.

1
The Location-based World

Location-based services (**LBS**) are pioneering and revolutionary services that have taken the Internet world by storm. The exponential growth of *smartphones* has led to increased demands for location-aware apps. The popular technology news blog `Gigaom.com` predicts that by the year 2016, LBS will be worth $10 billion. You can read the full report at:

```
http://gigaom.com/2011/06/09/location-based-services-worth-10b-
by-2016/
```

Location-based services are a revolutionary, yet still fresh-from-the-oven, breed of services that have grown tremendously to carve themselves a new industry in just a few years. LBS is the next stage of evolution for search, on the Web and mobile, adding the location context (where am I or things around me?) to search. To quote from Wikipedia on the definition of LBS:

> *"A location-based service (LBS) is an information and entertainment service, accessible with mobile devices through the mobile network and utilizing the ability to make use of the geographical position (read Geocodes or Latitude / Longitude) of the mobile device."*

You may have already used LBS when you use Twitter, Facebook, or when you visit **hyperlocal** web pages such as `CitySeekr.com`, `Yelp.com`, `Qype.co.uk`, and `Eventful.com` to find the top venues in the city or events happening in your city. Want to know how location is determined? Continue reading the chapter to understand the different methods of location detection, and which one is the right choice for you.

In this chapter we shall understand:

- Location-based services
- Buzzwords in the LBS industry

- Applications of LBS and common use cases
- How Microsoft uses LBS in Windows Phone 7.5 devices
- **Global Positioning System (GPS)**
- Indoor and outdoor navigation with GPS

Understanding location-based services

The concept of location-based services refers to services that integrate a mobile device's location with other topical information, to provide additional value to users. Consider a weather app that shows weather information for all of the United States of America cities. For a user living in San Francisco, this behemoth of information is not very helpful unless he can see the exact weather information for his city. This is achieved by mashing up the weather information with the user's location (generally obtained using a GPS system).

Another example of LBS is **local search websites** such as `CitySeekr.com` that presents a user with hyperlocal (read local, nearby, or neighborhood-centered) information about hotels, restaurants, shopping and entertainment venues that makes the user feel connected with the type of information shown to him/her. Still another example is the integrated Bing search in your Windows Phone 7.5 based phone (Nokia Lumia 800 in our case), which fetches the search request for `hotels in san francisco` with the location angle as well as regular web and image search, as shown in the following screenshot:

The core requirement for LBS is GPS (this will be covered in more detail shortly), a space-based satellite navigation system developed and maintained by the United States of America. Other countries also have similar systems; Russia has the Russian **Global Navigation Satellite System** (**GLONASS**) and Europe has the **Galileo** positioning system. India and China are working on their own positioning system as well, but GPS remains the most popular and preferred choice for device makers and application developers worldwide.

Anyone can use GPS freely by using either a Personal Navigation Device (Garmin, TomTom), an in-car navigation system (Ford SYNC), or using a smartphone.

On the mobile front, LBS also uses Bing, Google Maps, and other cartographic API services extensively (even in cases where the device does not support GPS). This is done using rich map data and geocoding services. Using geocoding and smart algorithms, a user's position can be guessed or approximated. Mobile operating systems such as Windows Phone 7.5 further the cause of LBS by integrating location into the core OS, where the location can be fetched, used, and updated by all applications.

Microsoft Windows Phone 7.5 (code name **Mango**) supports a Location Service Architecture that can obtain location data from the cellular network, **Assisted GPS** (**A-GPS**) that uses the network's data connection in case of weak GPS signals, as well as Microsoft's own Wi-Fi location database providing developers with a plethora of location tools and APIs to work with.

In short, LBS can be described as a combination of two services: location providers and location consumers, with GPS, A-GPS, and Windows Phone 7.5 Location API as the location providers, and GPS receivers, Windows Phone 7.5 devices, and websites as the consumers of location data.

Buzzwords in the location-based industry

As the book deals with Windows Phone location-aware apps, it is a good time to understand the following buzzwords and key terms used in the location-based industry:

- **Global Positioning System** (GPS): A satellite system that provides global navigation data including location and time.

- **Global Navigation Satellite System** (GLONASS): Russian navigation system.

- **Assisted GPS** (**A-GPS**): A mobile network assisted GPS system that uses the mobile network as a fall-back in areas of poor GPS coverage.

- **Geographic Information System (GIS)**: A system for storing, processing, and retrieving geographically-aware data, in addition to using user interface (usually raster map images) for easier management. A GIS typically involves both hardware and software.

- **Spatial database**: A database management system that is used for storing, querying, and fetching geotagged data, used in conjunction with GIS for data management.

- **Geocodes**: The latitude and longitude pair used to refer to a point on the earth's surface.

- **Geocoding**: The process of converting text addresses to geocodes using geocoding services such as GeoNames or Bing Maps API.

- **Reverse geocoding**: The process of converting geocodes to text addresses.

- **Geofencing**: The process of device-based alerts or notifications when entering a virtual geographical area. This geographic area can be a block, a lane, a neighborhood, a city, and so on, based on the application logic.

- **Check-ins**: These have been made popular by startup companies such as Foursquare and Footfeed. Checking-in refers to the process of confirming that you actually entered/checked-in to a place via a mobile phone app.

- **Geotagging**: The process of assigning geocodes (latitude-longitude pair values) to any news article, blog post, twitter tweet, or any other web action so that the location-based searches can be performed on them.

- **Location-based advertising (LBA)**: A new paradigm in web and mobile ads that are triggered by the location of the mobile device. Location-specific adverts for deals, events, movies, shopping, and restaurants offers are all possible with LBA.

- **Augmented reality (AR)**: AR is an exciting visual manipulation (augmentation) of the real-world environment (usually captured via mobile phone camera), combined with computer-generated (location-based) multimedia elements (pictures, audio, videos, 3D animation) usually in real time, giving users the perception of superimposition of computer-generated elements onto the real world.

- **HTML5**: The new version of the HyperText Markup Language that is under heavy development at W3C, and at browser companies such as Mozilla, Apple, Google, and Microsoft. HTML5 is poised to bring in a new and better way of writing HTML pages using standardized tags, which not only helps the web developers maintain code reusability but also makes it easy for search engines to semantically extract information from such HTML5 websites.

Applications of LBS and common use cases

The primary use of location-based services combined with GPS was and will remain the same: *Navigation*. There are new and exciting (and sometimes crazy!) ideas being implemented using LBS every other day. Research and Markets (http://www.researchandmarkets.com/) has predicted a market of US $10 billion for the LBS industry in 2015, from $2.8 billion in 2010. GigaOM (http://gigaom.com), a technology blog by Silicon Alley veteran Om Malik, has similar views on the LBS industry. Each year new location-based startup companies are being formed to bridge the gap between the vast information on the Internet and its availability for the local consumers/users.

Government and military, navigation, commercial industries such as advertising, social networks and web portals are the primary consumers of location-based services. GPS in fact was funded by the US **Department of Defense** (**DOD**) and still is maintained by DOD. It was initially designed for military use; in the late 1980s and early 1990s it was opened up for civilian use. Let us review the common use cases:

- **Military**: The US military uses GPS for navigation purposes including troops' movement. Target-tracking weapons use GPS to track their targets. Military aircrafts and missiles use GPS in various forms.

- **Government**: The government uses GPS for emergency services such as the US 9-1-1 service, which uses GPS to identify the caller's location quickly and provide emergency services on time.

- **Commercial**: Navigational GPS units that provide car owners with directions to destinations are the biggest commercial users of GPS. Air traffic control, seaport control, freight management, car and transport tracking, and Yellow Pages data management (local search) are other commercial uses of GPS.

 GPS is also used for time synchronization. The precision provided by GPS improves the time data by 40 billionths of a second.

How Microsoft uses LBS in Windows Phone 7.5

Microsoft's Windows Phone 7.5 (Mango) is a fresh new approach to mobile operating systems and user interfaces. In fact Microsoft has got good reviews from every quarter of the mobile phone world. What's different with Windows Phone is the emphasis on an integrated user experience rather than apps. The Metro user interface is clean, engaging, exciting, and different. Keeping the interface relevant and inclusive for the users, Microsoft has kept *location* as a compulsory hardware requirement for all Windows Phone handset manufacturers. This also signifies the important role of location in current and future Windows Phones. See *Hardware Specifications for Windows Phone* at:

```
http://msdn.microsoft.com/en-us/library/ff637514(v=vs.92).aspx
```

Let us now understand how Microsoft uses LBS in Windows Phone 7.5. As we learnt earlier, all WP7.5 phones have A-GPS and Wi-Fi capabilities built in the phone. This coupled with the **Microsoft Location Service** completes the location hardware and software required to build our location-aware apps!

Microsoft Location Service

In order to use the location APIs in your WP7.5 application, you need to include the `System.Device.Location` assembly in your application. Before you can use location in your app, make sure your device has **location** enabled; if not, you can enable it from the **SETTINGS** page on your WP7.5 Phone, as shown in the following screenshots from our Nokia Lumia 800:

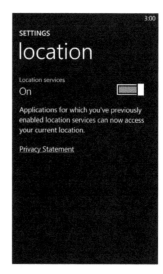

The `GeoCoordinateWatcher` class is the class which exposes the Windows Phone Location Service. It contains methods for both:

- Getting location information on demand
- Sending location information on position change or status change

Lastly, as with all mobile phone platforms, Microsoft has bundled an excellent **location sensor simulator** with the Windows Phone 7.1 SDK, which can be used to simulate location via live real-time values as well as saved values as shown in the following screenshot:

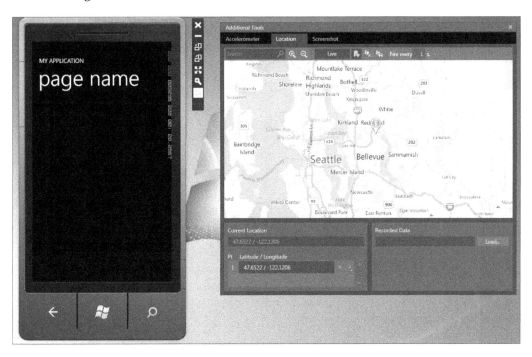

Behind location-based services – GPS

Let's learn a bit more on GPS as it powers all the current LBS implementations. If you are building the next generation navigation software or your own mapping applications, it is the right time to know more about GPS and how it works, so that it helps you make key decisions for your application.

GPS has three major components as shown in the next diagram (diagram courtesy Jörg Roth: `http://www.wireless-earth.de/jr_eng.html`): user segment (GPS receivers, mobile phones, car navigation units), space segment (24 satellites in orbit), and the GPS control segment having a base on Earth with the **Master Control Station** (**MCS**) in Colorado Springs, Colorado (so now you know where to head to get a clear signal!)

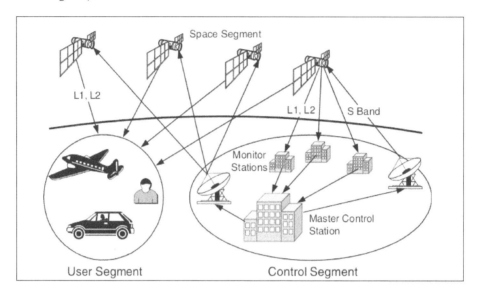

User segment

The user segment comprises of the GPS receivers embedded in millions of pieces of military equipment, almost all cell phones these days, aircraft and car navigation systems.

Space segment

The space segment comprises of the satellites orbiting Earth. The 24 satellites move in six different orbits around Earth at a distance of 20,200 km.

The satellites move in a manner that at every point of the earth's surface at least five and at most eleven satellites are visible over the horizon, for maximum accuracy.

Control segment

The control segment is the base on earth that controls the functioning of the GPS satellites and passes on the administrative commands such as correcting the satellite orbit and internal data. Several monitoring stations receive the satellite signals based on their location; they are synced with atomic clocks to calculate the correction data. This corrected data is then sent to the Master Control Station.

Push and pull methods of location services

Location-based service implementations are either based on **push services** or **pull services**, depending on the way location information is retrieved.

Push service

Push services imply that the user receives location information without having to actively or continuously keep requesting it. However, the user's consent is acquired beforehand. For example, the navigation software in your car will require your consent to use your location information when you switch it on, however, as you drive your car around town, your new location will automatically be acquired via push services.

Some more examples of push services include the Emergency Alert System (in case of terror attacks) and location-based advertising apps on your phone that notify you with deals, messages, and alerts on entering a new city or town.

Pull service

Pull services work on the on demand principle; your apps would request location information from the network on demand. For example, if you use the Local Scout app (`http://www.microsoft.com/windowsphone/en-us/howto/wp7/web/local-scout.aspx`) on your Nokia Lumia 800, the Windows Phone 7.5 OS would request location information when it loads. Also you can change the location via the **Settings** page of the app. This way, the application pulls location information when it needs to, and not continuously.

In the forthcoming chapters, we will be building apps mostly using the pull services, including a local news app and an events app that will pull location information on demand, and mash it with information retrieved via web services.

This type of location retrieval is also good for the battery power consumption of your phone, as GPS positioning involves a significant amount of battery power.

Life without GPS: Wi-Fi based location detection

There are alternate ways to detect location from mobile phone devices using their Wi-Fi MAC addresses (access points that connect to the internet) to determine/approximate the user's location.

Wi-Fi based positioning returns the approximate location, which may not be the exact latitude-longitude pair, but it does not provide a high level of precision.

Companies such as Skyhook Wireless and Google (with Google Latitude) were the first to provide this service. Microsoft launched a similar service under the "Managed Driving" name in July 2011, which uses cars driven around cities collecting Wi-Fi information broadcasted by public Wi-Fi access points. This coupled with location obtained from Windows mobile devices completes the data aggregation loop for Microsoft's own positioning database.

Skyhook Wireless location is pretty much public, with provisions for end users to add their location data to its database via a web interface, which is then available to all implementations of Skyhook wireless API users. Their database uses over 250 million Wi-Fi access points and cellular tower information for location analysis. Skyhook deploys data collection vehicles to conduct the access point survey, similarly to the Google Street View cars. The accuracy provided by Skyhook Wireless is 10 meters. To know more about Skyhook Wireless coverage go to:

```
http://www.skyhookwireless.com/howitworks/coverage.php
```

To get an idea on how Skyhook Wireless works:

1. Visit `http://loki.com/findme`.
2. Install the Java add-on it prompts.
3. Wait for a few seconds and you should see your location detected; if not you can submit your Wi-Fi Access Point to Skyhook Wireless at:

    ```
    http://www.skyhookwireless.com/howitworks/submit_ap.php
    ```

The following screenshot shows my location on loki.com:

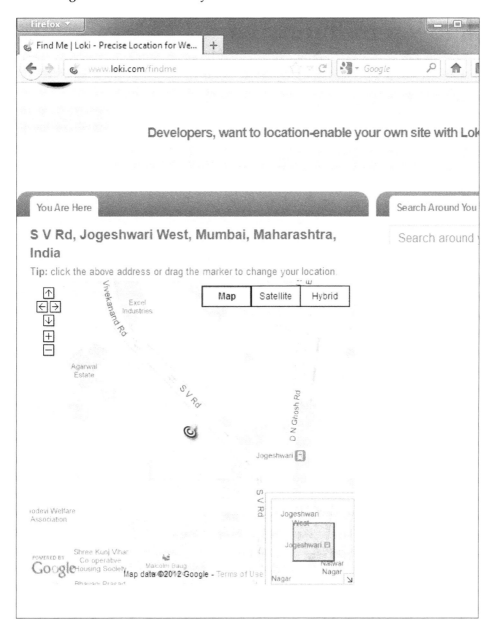

Life without GPS: Cell-ID positioning and cell tower triangulation

Low-cost or price-sensitive mobile phones often come without GPS or Wi-Fi. These phones are meant to do what mobile phones are intended to be used for – *Talk*. However, location of the user can still be detected on such phones using cellular towers. **Cell-ID positioning** and **cell tower triangulation** are two different ways to get location information from cell towers. Cell-ID result accuracy is only 200-1000 meters; hence it is used as the last option for most location-detection methodologies.

Cell-ID positioning uses your mobile network's cell tower to find your location. This involves the nearest tower to which your phone connects when you place calls. Cell tower triangulation on the other hand uses all the cellular towers around you to calculate your position, based on the signal strength your phone receives from each of the towers. Triangulation is more accurate, however it is a slower process.

It is important to acknowledge privacy and security issues for end users while developing your applications and choosing the type of location-detection and storage. In July 2001, CNET discovered that Microsoft had collected the location data from millions of smartphones, laptops, and other Wi-Fi devices, which was easily accessible on the Web (`http://news.cnet.com/8301-31921_3-20085028-281/microsofts-web-map-exposes-phone-pc-locations/`). Microsoft rectified it in response to the CNET report (`http://arstechnica.com/microsoft/news/2011/08/microsoft-locks-down-wi-fi-location-service-after-privacy-concerns.ars`) but this has been an eye-opener for user privacy and security watchers.

Life without GPS: Bing Maps API

Bing Maps provides a REST API for creating a static map with pushpins, geocoding an address, and creating routes. There are a plethora of options available for Microsoft lovers (`http://msdn.microsoft.com/en-us/library/dd877180.aspx`) ranging from Ajax controls to iOS controls for using Bing Maps in your application. We will, however, use the REST API to determine the user's location (when Wi-Fi and cellular radio is not available to determine location).

Specifically we will use the Bing Maps API to convert a user address into location; this process is known as geocoding, as described earlier. Bing Maps uses these coordinates to plot the locations on a map. The Bing Maps API provides an option for both geocoding and reverse geocoding.

To illustrate a simple REST API call from the Bing Maps API that finds location by a given address, see `http://msdn.microsoft.com/en-us/library/ff701715.aspx`. The Geocoding API is consumed by the following API call:

```
http://dev.virtualearth.net/REST/v1/Locations/
US/adminDistrict/postalCode/locality/
addressLine?includeNeighborhood=includeNeighborhood&key=BingMapsKey,
```
where the output can be either JSON or XML, and the parameters can be either of the following:

Parameters	Description
adminDistrict	Typically a US state.
postalCode	US zip code.
Locality	City name.
addressLine	Street address.
includeNeighborhood	For including neighborhood data in response. This value can be either 0 or 1.
BingMapsKey	Key obtained from `https://www.bingmapsportal.com/`.

An example geocoding request for Microsoft Corporation office at Mountain View, San Francisco, CA, USA is constructed as:

`http://dev.virtualearth.net/REST/v1/Locations/US/CA/94043/San Francisco/1065 La Avenida St?o=xml&key=xxxxxxxxxxxxxxxx`, where xxxxxxxxxxxxxxxx is the Bing Maps API key you obtained from `https://www.bingmapsportal.com/`. This API call returns the following results:

Our interest lies is in the `<Latitude>` and `<Longitude>` XML nodes, which hold the location value for the address we specified. If you do not have the exact address, you can use the **Find a location by Query** API call of the Bing Maps API, where the input can be any query string. Depending upon your app's targeted region, construct the right REST call. As they say, "Read the documentation carefully".

Understanding indoor and outdoor navigation

Navigation functionality in cars, airplanes, railways, and mobile phones is mostly optimized for on-the-move functionality. It assumes that the user of such services tends to exhibit movement from one place to another with time. This is classified as outdoor navigation, implying navigation done outside homes, offices, malls, and any place not confined to a building or large area.

This is where indoor navigation sets in. Although GPS and other positioning systems have high coverage and accuracy, they fail when you are indoors, in a mall, or a shopping complex; even airport lounges, stadiums, and office complexes because the radio signals from GPS transmitters cannot penetrate walls. Indoor navigation works in such places using techniques dissimilar to outdoor navigation; in short, there is no GPS for indoor navigation.

There are various implementations of indoor navigation, some using infrared techniques, some using radio signals (RFID), and another implementation using ultrasound. Companies like Visioglobe (`http://visioglobe.com`) offer an SDK for indoor navigational purposes. Another company – WiFiSLAM — is building a Wi-Fi based solution. While the market for indoor navigation is quite big and the outlook for growth is very positive, the implementation and standardization is at a very nascent stage, partly due to the fact that a generic solution that fits all is not possible for indoor navigation. Also, interactive kiosks at malls, airports, and convention centers solve the problem of information management for visitors.

Summary

In this introductory chapter, we have identified how location-based services work, the buzzwords behind all things location and the importance of GPS.

Specifically, we discovered location-based services and their applications in the real world, how Microsoft uses location in its Windows Phone 7.5 devices, and GPS and non-GPS based solutions for location. We also discussed new potential in LBS markets, that of indoor navigation.

Now that we've got our feet grounded in location, we can move to the next chapter that covers Windows Phone 7.5 Location Services!

2
Using Location in Windows Phone 7.5

Having looked at **location-based services** (**LBS**) and after getting a quick look at Microsoft's Location Service in *Chapter 1*, *The Location-based World*, we will now explore the Microsoft Location Service in abundant detail in this chapter, as well as build a simple "Hello Location" app for our Windows Phone, modeled after the "Hello World" paradigm!

This chapter covers:

- Introduction to Windows Phone 7.5
- Overview of Windows Phone Location Service
- Starting and using the Location Service
- Building a Hello Location application
- Working with the Windows Phone location simulator

Introduction to Windows Phone 7.5

Windows Phone 7.5 (codenamed **Mango**) is a visually appealing upgrade to Windows Phone 7, and a complete rewrite-from-scratch for the ageing Windows Mobile 6.5 (remember the phones with the **Start** menu!). With iPhone and Android ushering in a new era of *smartphones* focusing on simplicity and user interface, Microsoft was a bit late in the game with its offerings. However, the launch of Windows Phone 7.5 (internal version 7.1) saw Microsoft coming back into the arena with a refreshing new UI, tighter integration with Office, social hub, Xbox LIVE, and a bag full of other goodies.

Apps can be downloaded from the integrated **Windows Phone Marketplace**. The **home screen** is different as well; you are no longer thrown with tons of app icons on it, instead the home screen on the Windows Phone is an iconic grid of **Tiles** (that can be customized). Each of these Tiles can be updated in real time, so there is no need to manually open an application and update them. For example, think of a photo tile that updates itself whenever there is a new photo available from the user's subscribed channels. More on Tiles soon; to get a feel of the home screen, see the following screenshot:

Microsoft's partnership with the mobile industry goliath Nokia saw the emergence of great smartphones powered by Nokia's excellent hardware coupled with Microsoft's decades of knowledge and research in software, particularly Windows.

The current Nokia WP7.5 handset models are listed as follows:

- Nokia Lumia 800 (We use this device as the test device for our examples and apps in the book)
- Nokia Lumia 710 (A trimmed version of Lumia 800)
- Nokia Lumia 900
- Nokia Lumia 610 (Entry-level WP7.5 Phone)

Let us now look at some of the key functionality in Windows Phone 7.5 Mango:

- Live Tiles
- Panorama control
- Pivot control
- App Connect

Live Tiles

Live Tiles are Microsoft's killer feature, which clearly differentiates it from the iPhones and the Androids. Live Tiles allow you to pin applications to the home screen for live updates. Any application apart from the default phone dialer, e-mail, and messaging can use the Live Tiles functionality to allow for live updates when the application is pinned to the home screen.

Technically Tiles are 37x37 pixel components that includes the application title, background image, icon, and a count. You can also have a double-sided tile! Tiles can be updated in two different ways: via the application logic and via push notifications through the Microsoft Notification Service.

Panorama control

Panorama-based applications offer a unique view of content by providing a long horizontal canvas to the app. The user can scroll back and forth between the screens easily. The idea of a panorama app is to give the users a sneak peak of the next/previous screens thereby leading to more content view.

The next screenshot depicts an example of a panorama-based application including a background image scaled horizontally to fit each screen differently, thus giving a pleasant experience when using the app.

Pivot control

Pivot-based applications are similar to panorama controls, except for the fact that a pivot takes up the full screen and can handle a large number of pivot items (Microsoft recommends only up to *four* screens for panorama control). Unlike the panorama control, pivots do not show a preview of the next screen. The search on the Windows Phone 7.5 devices uses the pivot control, as shown in the following screenshot:

App Connect

App Connect is a new way of discovering apps (apart from the Windows Marketplace), via the search experience on the phone. With App Connect, users can launch an application directly from the Bing search results display. This makes it easier for users to search the data and find apps that can use that data. For example, if you are searching for foursquare on your Windows Phone, you will get the first result as the app itself. See the following screenshot:

Tools for Windows Phone 7.5 developers

The Windows Phone SDK 7.1 (the SDK version is 7.1 while the marketed version is 7.5) available for download at `http://www.microsoft.com/download/en/details.aspx?displaylang=en&id=27570` includes the following tools to get you started with building apps for Windows Phone:

- Visual Studio 2010 Express for Windows Phone
- Microsoft Expression Blend 4 for Windows Phone
- XAML

Download the `vm_web2.exe` file as shown in the following screenshot and double-click on it to start the installation:

Accept the **License Agreement** as shown in the following screenshot:

Next select the **Install Now** button to continue with the default installation profile as shown in the next screenshot. This method of installation should be fine for most use cases.

Continue to download the files and finish the installation. Once the installation is over, you should see **Visual Studio 2010 Express for Windows Phone** and **Microsoft Expression Blend 4** installed in the **Start** menu.

Visual Studio 2010 Express for Windows Phone

Visual Studio 2010 Express for Windows Phone provides all the tools required to build your Windows Phone applications. From Silverlight applications to XNA-based games, you can build multiple types of applications using the same IDE. The bundled Windows Phone Emulator helps you test your applications before submitting to the Marketplace. Application developers can work with C# or VB.NET to code their applications. The following screenshot shows what the main window of the studio looks:

It is a good idea to register the product as soon as you are done with the installation.

Microsoft Expression Blend 4 for Windows Phone

The Windows Phone 7.1 SDK also includes a design tool called **Expression Blend** (version 4) that allows for designing Windows Phone applications. Think it of as Photoshop for Windows Phone developers! However Expression Blend works with the full project solution, so you can design your applications and run the app in the emulator right within Expression Blend.

XAML

Windows Phone app development using Silverlight involves the use of the **Extensible Application Markup Language** (**XAML**). XAML has an XML-based structure for defining the look and feel for Silverlight-based applications. XAML controls in Silverlight communicate with our code (C# or VB.NET) via the control **properties**.

Windows Phone Location Service

Location information in your Windows Phone applications is managed by the Windows Phone Location Service, which allows you to use your device's Wi-Fi, GPS, or cellular network to determine location. As we discussed earlier, Microsoft lays strong emphasis on location, so much that it is a basic hardware requirement for all Windows Phones.

The main class that handles the Location Service is the `GeoCoordinateWatcher` class. Perform the following steps and make sure you import the DLL in your solution:

1. Create a new **Windows Phone Application** project in **Microsoft Visual Studio 2010 Express for Windows Phone** by selecting the **Visual C#** template. **Name** it `PhoneApp1` as shown in the following screenshot:

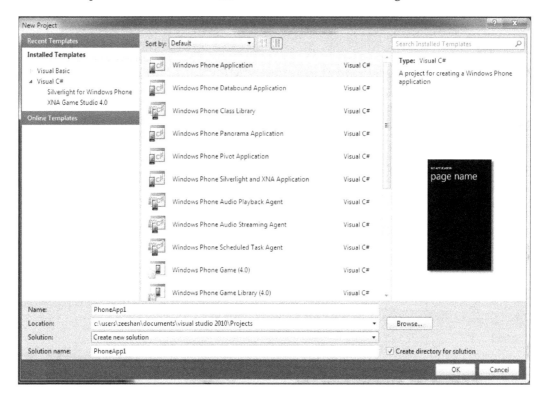

2. Now select your project name in **Solution Explorer**, and add the `System.Device` reference as shown in the following screenshot:

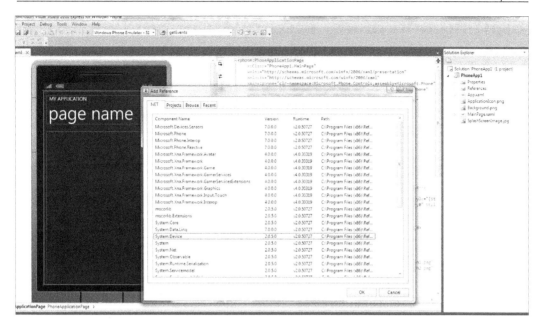

3. In your `MainPage.xaml.cs` file import the following location namespace by using the `using` keyword:

```
using System.Device.Location;
```

Downloading the example code

You can download the example code files for all Packt books you have purchased from your account at `http://www.packtpub.com`. If you purchased this book elsewhere, you can visit `http://www.packtpub.com/support` and register to have the files e-mailed directly to you.

```
MainPage.xaml.cs ×  MainPage.xaml
PhoneApp1.MainPage
using System;
using System.Collections.Generic;
using System.Linq;
using System.Net;
using System.Windows;
using System.Windows.Controls;
using System.Windows.Documents;
using System.Windows.Input;
using System.Windows.Media;
using System.Windows.Media.Animation;
using System.Windows.Shapes;
using Microsoft.Phone.Controls;
using System.Device.Location;

namespace PhoneApp1
{
    public partial class MainPage : PhoneApplicationPag
```

Starting and using the Location Service

Now that we know how to import the Location Service, let us now learn how to start using it.

To start the Location Service, the `Start` method of the `GeoCoordinateWatcher` class needs to be called. Continuing from our previous example, open the `MainPage.xaml.cs` file and create a variable of type `GeoCoordinateWatcher` in your `MainPage()` constructor as:

```
var locationManager = new GeoCoordinateWatcher();
```

And declare the `locationManager` variable in the global scope, by declaring it as a field right after the class initialization.

```
public partial class MainPage : PhoneApplicationPage
{
    GeoCoordinateWatcher locationManager;
```

Now we call the `Start` method as:

```
locationManager.Start();
```

To quickly get the latitude/longitude data (assuming the application can access location information), add two `TextBlock` elements to your main XAML file (`MainPage.xaml`) and name them `latitudeText` and `longitudeText` respectively. This is shown in the following screenshot:

Add the following code to `MainPage.xaml.cs` in the `MainPage()` constructor, after the `locationManager.Start()` line:

```
latitudeText.Text=
  locationManager.Position.Location.Latitude.ToString("0.000");
longitudeText.Text =
  locationManager.Position.Location.Longitude.ToString("0.000");
```

Running the example in the emulator will produce the following result:

In the previous example, we assumed that the GPS or other location-determining hardware was ready to return the location information as soon as we requested it. However, this is not true in a real-world scenario, GPS devices may take a few seconds to get a good signal in a remote place. The `GeoCoordinateWatcher` class implements the `StatusChanged` event to handle this, returning the status (of type `GeoPositionStatus`), which could be any of the following based on the device's status:

Status	Description
Initialising	The Windows Phone Location Service is trying to acquire data
Ready	The Location Service is ready with data
Disabled	Service disabled or not supported
NoData	The device can fetch location information, but no data available (due to poor reception or otherwise)

We define the `StatusChanged` event handler function immediately after creating the `locationManager` variable in the `MainPage()` constructor as:

```
locationManager.StatusChanged += new
  EventHandler<GeoPositionStatusChangedEventArgs>
  (locationManager_getStatus);
```

`locationManager_getStatus` is our custom-defined function where we handle the statuses for the `GeoCoordinateWatcher` class, which is defined as:

```
void locationManager_getStatus(object sender,
  GeoPositionStatusChangedEventArgs e)
{
  switch (e.Status)
  {
    case GeoPositionStatus.Initializing:
      statusText.Text = "Loading ...";
      break;

    case GeoPositionStatus.Ready:
      latitudeText.Text =
       locationManager.Position.Location.Latitude.ToString();
      longitudeText.Text =
       locationManager.Position.Location.Longitude.ToString();
      statusText.Text = "Location Available";
      break;

    case GeoPositionStatus.Disabled:
      statusText.Text = "Disabled";
      break;

    case GeoPositionStatus.NoData:
      statusText.Text = "No Data at this time";
      break;
  }// end of switch
} // end of locationManager_getStatus
```

In most cases, you should be able to get the location; however, there could be two reasons for location being disabled:

- The application does not have the permission for location (lock-down by carrier/ app developer or country-wise restrictions)
- The device can access location, but the user has disabled the location services from the phone setting

We cannot help in the first case; however, in the second case we can use the `Permission` property of the `GeoCoordinateWatcher` class. Modify the `GeoPositionStatus.disabled` case from the previous example to the following one:

```
case GeoPositionStatus.Disabled:
  if (locationManager.Permission == GeoPositionPermission.Denied)
  {
    statusText.Text = "User has disabled location settings";
  }
  else
    statusText.Text = "Disabled";
  break;
```

To display the status of the Location Service, we added one more `TextBlock` to the UI (via the `MainPage.xaml` file) and named it `statusText`, and placed it near the footer of the app as shown in the following screenshot:

There is no way to disable the location settings on the emulator yet, so we tested this example on the phone itself. The following screenshot shows how the application will behave with location settings turned off (see *Chapter 1, The Location-based World* on how to turn location settings on/off):

You can also specify accuracy for the GeoCoordinateWatcher object by passing an argument of type GeoPositionAccuracy. There are two accuracy levels:

- **High**: For highest accurate positioning information. It uses high battery power consumption.

- **Default**: Optimized for power and performance.

We will modify our GeoCoordinateWatcher object to use the high accuracy level by using the following arguments at the object creation time:

```
locationManager = new
  GeoCoordinateWatcher(GeoPositionAccuracy.High);
```

It is also a good practice to use the Stop() method wherever possible to turn off the Location Service when not needed, to maximize the battery life of the device.

You can find this example project in the code files for the book under Chapter 2, titled PhoneApp1.

Your application must inform users on how location information is used in your app. This is part of the privacy policy Microsoft ensures for applications using location data. If you fail to provide the same, the application might be rejected.

Continuous monitoring of the Location Service

In our previous example we saw how to fetch the location data when the service is ready. We saw a simple way to access the location data from the GeoCoordinateWatcher object; however, there is another event exposed by the GeoCoordinateWatcher class – the PositionChanged event that is fired when the location service detects a change in the position of the Windows Phone device.

Let us now build our Hello Location example that uses both the StatusChanged and PositionChanged events:

1. Open Visual Studio 2010 Express and create a new project by clicking on the **File | New Project** menu option. Provide the application name as Hello Location as shown in the following screenshot:

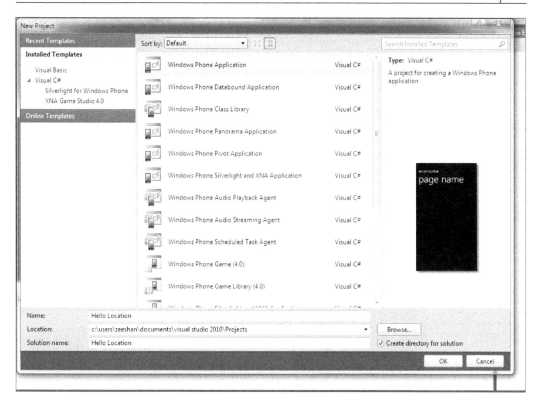

2. Make sure to select your Target Windows Phone Platform as 7.1 as shown in the following screenshot:

3. Add the `System.Device` reference library to your project and import it in your `MainPage.xaml.cs` file by adding the following line:

```
using System.Device.Location;
```

4. Do not forget to define the location manager in the global class context:

```
GeoCoordinateWatcher locationManager;
```

5. We add two buttons to our UI, one for starting the location service and another for stopping the same. We also add four `TextBlocks`, two for the latitude/longitude labels and two more for their respective values. The following screenshot shows how our UI should now look:

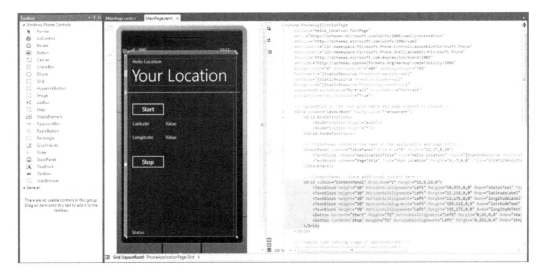

6. Note the XAML view for your project and the highlighted text shown in the previous screenshot. Make sure you align the UI elements properly using the `Margin` property. Name the elements properly so that you can access them in your code.

```
<Grid x:Name="ContentPanel" Grid.Row="1"Margin="12,0,12,0">
  <TextBlock Height="30" HorizontalAlignment="Left"
   Margin="10,575,0,0" Name="statusText" Text="Status: "
   VerticalAlignment="Top" Width="444" />
  <TextBlock Height="30" HorizontalAlignment="Left"
   Margin="12,118,0,0" Name="latitudeLabel" Text="Latitude: "
   VerticalAlignment="Top" />
  <TextBlock Height="30" HorizontalAlignment="Left"
   Margin="12,175,0,0" Name="longitudeLabel" Text="Longitude: "
   VerticalAlignment="Top" />
  <TextBlock Height="30" HorizontalAlignment="Left"
```

```
      Margin="155,118,0,0" Name="latitudeText" Text="Value"
      VerticalAlignment="Top" />
     <TextBlock Height="30" HorizontalAlignment="Left"
      Margin="155,175,0,0" Name="longitudeText" Text="Value"
      VerticalAlignment="Top" />
     <Button Content="Start" Height="72"
      HorizontalAlignment="Left" Margin="0,35,0,0"
      Name="startButton" VerticalAlignment="Top" Width="160"
      Click="startButton_Click" />
     <Button Content="Stop" Height="72" HorizontalAlignment="Left"
      Margin="0,256,0,0" Name="stopButton" VerticalAlignment="Top"
      Width="160" Click="stopButton_Click" />
   </Grid>
```

7. Note the `Click="startButton_Click"` and `Click="stopButton_Click"` code in XAML shown in the previous step. These are click event functions that are called when the user hits the start and stop buttons. From your UI, double-clicking on the buttons will open up the code editor for modifying these function calls.

```
private void startButton_Click(object sender,
 RoutedEventArgs e)
{
   locationManager.Start();
}


private void stopButton_Click(object sender,
 RoutedEventArgs e)
{
   locationManager.Stop();
}
```

8. We saw the `StatusChanged` event of the `GeoCoordinateWatcher` class earlier, now we will implement the `PositionChanged` event. In your `MainPage()` constructor, after creating an object `locationManager` of type `GeoCoordinaeWatcher`, we declare the `PositionChanged` event as:

```
locationManager = new
 GeoCoordinateWatcher(GeoPositionAccuracy.High);
locationManager.StatusChanged += new
 EventHandler<GeoPositionStatusChangedEventArgs>
 (locationManager_getStatus);
locationManager.PositionChanged += new
 EventHandler<GeoPositionChangedEventArgs<GeoCoordinate>>
 (locationManager_getPosition);
```

9. Note, for our Hello Location example, we define the accuracy as high as shown in the previous code.

10. Now we define the `locationManager_getPosition` function as:

```
void locationManager_getPosition(object sender,
 GeoPositionChangedEventArgs<GeoCoordinate>newLoc)
{
  latitudeText.Text =
   newLoc.Position.Location.Latitude.ToString();
  longitudeText.Text =
   newLoc.Position.Location.Longitude.ToString();
}
```

11. The `locationManager_getPosition` function exposes the device's current location via the `<GeoCoordinate>` parameter in the function declaration. We use this in our implementation via the `newLoc` variable, and pass the current latitude and longitude values to the respective `TextBlock` for display.

12. Running the Hello Location example produces the following result:

13. Click on the **Start** button to get the location values from the device as shown in the following screenshot:

You can find this example project in the code files for the book under Chapter 2, titled Hello Location.

 We used the Nokia Lumia 800 skin on our emulator; get yours from http://www.developer.nokia.com/Community/ Wiki/How_to_use_skins_of_Nokia_Lumia_on_Windows_ Phone_emulator. For multiple skin choices head to http:// wp7emuskinswitcher.codeplex.com/, which allows you to switch skins for a couple of phones, and yes there is a white Nokia Lumia 800 skin too!

Working with the Windows Phone location simulator

Having played with our Hello Location example app, let us now dig more into the Windows Phone location simulator to understand how we can simulate location data in our application.

Open the Hello Location example and run it in Windows Phone Emulator. The Emulator comes with an **Additional Tools** sidebar, which is activated from the Emulator home screen via the **Additional Tools** button (**>>**) as shown in the following screenshot:

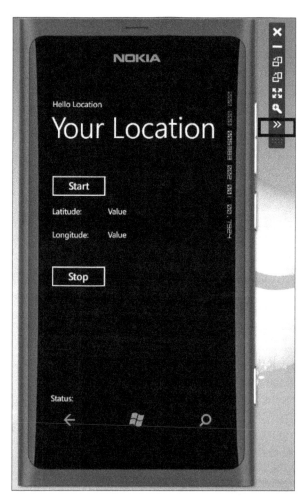

Within the **Additional Tools** sidebar open, select the **Location** tab, as shown in the following screenshot:

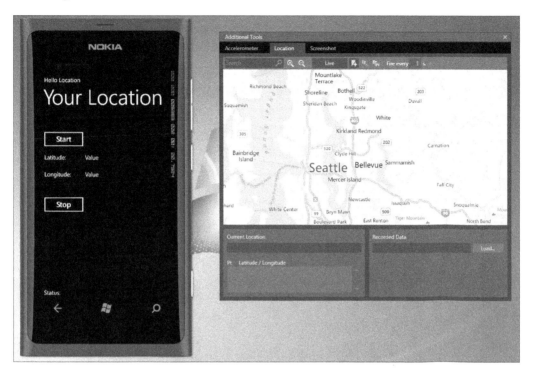

When you run the Hello Location example, the values you get for the latitude/longitude pair by default would be **47.64483** and **-122.141197**, which is Microsoft's Redmond office. Playing around with the location simulator and the Hello Location application side by side, you will find the location updates happen immediately on the Hello Location app.

You can also search for places using the search input box. A cool feature of the simulator is the ability to save the maps points you have added on the maps. This can be loaded back from the saved file or by manually adding points to simulate your app behavior, by loading the saved locations file (Locations.xml in our case) and hitting the **Play all points** button as shown in the following screenshot:

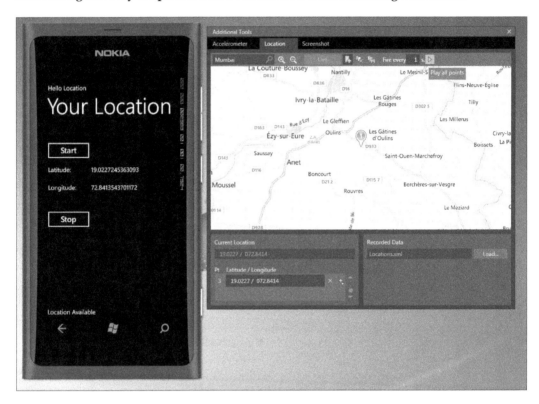

The Location.xml file is shown as follows; we added two different cities' latitude/longitude data to it and checked the Hello Location app against it.

```xml
<?xml version="1.0" encoding="utf-8"?>
<WindowsPhoneEmulator xmlns=
 "http://schemas.microsoft.com/WindowsPhoneEmulator/2009/08/
 SensorData">
  <SensorData>
    <Header version="1" />
    <GpsData latitude="48.8596434322625"
     longitude="1.49173867702484" />
    <GpsData latitude="48.645964012732"
     longitude="1.49723184108734" />
```

```
    <GpsData latitude="19.0227245363093"
      longitude="72.8413543701172" />
  </SensorData>
</WindowsPhoneEmulator>
```

Summary

In this chapter we got introduced to Windows Phone 7.5 and using location in our applications.

Specifically we covered an introduction to Windows Phone 7.5 followed by an overview of Windows Phone 7.5 Location Service—starting and using the Location Service. We also built a Hello Location app for Windows Phone. Lastly we looked at working with the location simulator.

In the next chapter we will explore how to use maps in our Windows Phone applications and then we will build some cool apps, so keep reading.

3
Using Maps in your Windows Phone App

Any book covering location is not complete without mentioning maps. Maps provide a great visual experience for location-based services. Maps are now a default feature on most smartphones as they provide a good graphical overview of information (usually geotagged data) around the user's location.

With custom pin markers and directions, maps also help users navigate to their destination easily. Most importantly maps give the user a feeling that "This place is around the next block, north from where I am standing," so decision-making happens quickly for the user.

In this chapter we shall cover the following topics:

- Understanding map geometry
- Overview of Windows Bing Maps Silverlight Control
- Using maps in your Windows Phone application – Hello Maps
- Using pushpins with maps
- Custom map pushpins
- Handling pushpin events
- Working with Bing Maps geocoding and reverse geocoding services
- Overview of Launchers and Choosers
- Using directions with Bing Maps directions task
- Performing local searches with `BingMapsTask`

Understanding map geometry

Windows Phone 7.5 supports two methods of map display in your mobile app:

- Bing Maps Silverlight Control for Windows Phone
- Bing Maps task Launcher

Before we delve into the methods, actions, and tasks of the Windows Phone Bing Maps Silverlight Control or the Bing Maps task Launcher, it is a good idea to get acquainted with the background of map geometry and how it works for Bing Maps. If you have a background in Computer Science, then you would be aware of keywords such as projection, trajectory, coordinate systems, raster and scalable graphics. If you are not from a Computer Science background, then a basic understanding of the Bing Maps API can be found at `http://msdn.microsoft.com/en-us/library/ff428643.aspx`. This should be good to get you started with Bing Maps.

Bing Maps uses the **Mercator projection** model of converting the Earth's sphere into a corresponding flat surface, grid-based, parallel map. In such a projection the longitude lines are parallel, and hence the land mass further from the equator tends to be distorted. However, the Mercator projection works well for navigational purposes, and therefore, despite the drawbacks, it is still used today.

The Mercator projection offers two compelling advantages:

- The map scale is constant around any position.
- Mercator projection is a cylindrical projection. North and south are straight up and down, while west and east are always left and right respectively. (This helps in keeping track of your course in navigation.)

The following diagrams should give you a good idea about the Mercator projection:

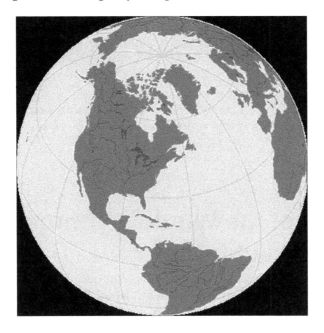

 Earth's surface as a sphere diagram courtesy Michael Pidwirny from `http://www.eoearth.org/article/` `Maps` and `http://www.physicalgeography.net/` `fundamentals/2a.html`.

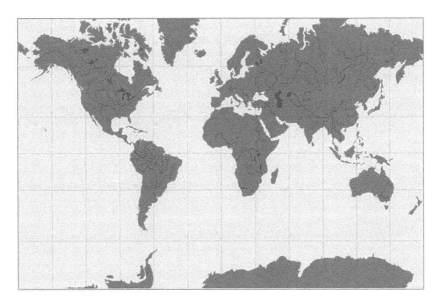

Mercator projection of the Earth's surface diagram courtesy Michael Pidwirny from `http://www.eoearth.org/article/Maps` and `http://www.physicalgeography.net/fundamentals/2a.html`.

The world map is pre-rendered at many different levels of detail and cut into **tiles** for quick retrieval. When you zoom in or zoom out on your Bing Maps, it is nothing but loading different tiles at different levels. To read more about the Bing Maps Tile System please see the following MSDN link:

`http://msdn.microsoft.com/en-us/library/bb259689.aspx`

Overview of the Windows Phone Bing Maps Silverlight Control

The Bing Maps Silverlight Control for Windows Phone 7.5 is a port of the desktop version of the Silverlight Map Control, which provides full mapping capabilities on the Windows Phone 7.5 device. Before using the Bing Maps control you need to get an application key from Microsoft's Bing Maps portal at: `https://www.bingmapsportal.com/`.

The `Microsoft.Phone.Controls.Maps` namespace contains the classes of the Bing Maps Silverlight Control for Windows Phone. Let us quickly see an example of using maps in our WP7.5 app.

Using maps in your Windows Phone 7.5 app – Hello Maps

Similar to the `Hello Location` application that we saw in *Chapter 2, Using Location in Windows Phone 7.5*, we will now create a new application titled `HelloMaps` that shows the Windows Phone Bing Maps Silverlight Control in action:

1. Launch **Microsoft Visual Studio 2010 Express for Windows Phone**.

2. Create a new Project from the **File | New Project** menu option and **Name** it `HelloMaps`.

3. Add the **Map** control to your app by selecting it from the **Toolbox**. Change the **Application Title** to `Hello Maps` and the **Page Title** to `Bing Maps`. Your project should now look like the following screenshot:

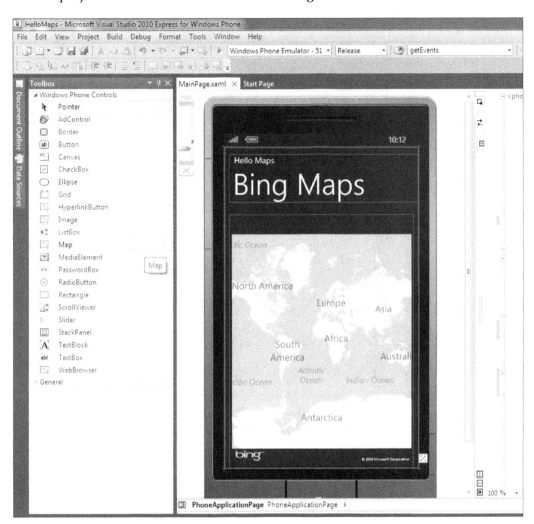

4. If you run the app now it will show the following output, as depicted in the next screenshot:

Invalid Credentials. Sign up for a developer account at:

`http://www.microsoft.com/maps/developers`

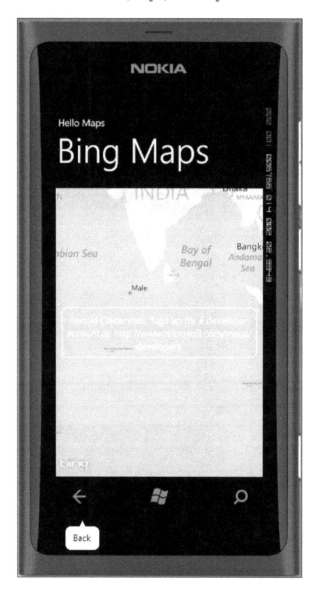

5. This is because we have not signed up for a map key from `https://www.bingmapsportal.com/`. Let's do so.

6. Visit `https://www.bingmapsportal.com/` and sign up or log in with your Windows Live ID. Create your application and store the map key in a safe place.

7. Now that we have our key, (for safety reason we assume xxxxxxxxxxxxxx as the key) let us initialize our **Map** control with the same.

8. Notice the XAML tag `<my:Map>` when you added the **Map** control to your application. Add the key we got from step 7 by using the `CredentialsProvider` attribute of the Bing Maps Silverlight Control. Also change the name of the map to `"myMap"`.

```
<Grid x:Name="ContentPanel" Grid.Row="1" Margin="12,0,12,0">
  <my:Map Height="595"
  CredentialsProvider="xxxxxxxxxxxxxx"
  HorizontalAlignment="Left" Margin="6,6,0,0" Name="myMap"
  VerticalAlignment="Top" Width="444" />
</Grid>
```

9. Running the app in the emulator now will not show the **Invalid Credentials** message we saw earlier.

10. Now let us make our application more exciting. We will add an Application Bar to our `Hello Maps` application that will allow us to choose the map mode: Road Mode or Aerial Mode.

11. In your `MainPage.xaml` uncomment the following lines that add a default application bar to your application:

```
<!--Sample code showing usage of ApplicationBar-->
<!--<phone:PhoneApplicationPage.ApplicationBar>
  <shell:ApplicationBar IsVisible="True" IsMenuEnabled="True">
    <shell:ApplicationBarIconButton
     IconUri="/Images/appbar_button1.png" Text="Button 1"/>
    <shell:ApplicationBarIconButton
     IconUri="/Images/appbar_button2.png" Text="Button 2"/>
    <shell:ApplicationBar.MenuItems>
      <shell:ApplicationBarMenuItem Text="MenuItem 1"/>
      <shell:ApplicationBarMenuItem Text="MenuItem 2"/>
    </shell:ApplicationBar.MenuItems>
  </shell:ApplicationBar>
</phone:PhoneApplicationPage.ApplicationBar>-->
```

12. Modify it to look like the following:

```
<phone:PhoneApplicationPage.ApplicationBar>
  <shell:ApplicationBar IsVisible="True" IsMenuEnabled="True">
    <shell:ApplicationBar.MenuItems>
      <shell:ApplicationBarMenuItem Text="Aerial Mode"/>
      <shell:ApplicationBarMenuItem Text="Road Mode"/>
    </shell:ApplicationBar.MenuItems>
  </shell:ApplicationBar>
</phone:PhoneApplicationPage.ApplicationBar>
```

13. Now we have seen in *Chapter 2, Using Location in Windows Phone 7.5* how to push click events from the XAML code to C#. With your code editor open, go to the `Aerial Mode` Application Bar Menu Item and before the `Text` property enter `Click=""`. **IntelliSense** will prompt you `<New Event Handler>` as shown in the following screenshot. Select it.

```
                      </Grid>

      <phone:PhoneApplicationPage.ApplicationBar>
            <shell:ApplicationBar IsVisible="True" IsMenuEnabled="True">
                <shell:ApplicationBar.MenuItems>
                    <shell:ApplicationBarMenuItem Click="" Text="Aerial Mode"/>
```

Bind event to a newly created method called 'ApplicationBarMenuItem_Click'. Use 'Navigate to Event Handler' to   <New Event Handler>
navigate to the newly created method.

```
      </phone:PhoneApplicationPage.ApplicationBar>

    </phone:PhoneApplicationPage>
```

14. Do the same for the other Application Bar Menu Item. Your code should now be as follows:

```
<shell:ApplicationBarMenuItem
 Click="ApplicationBarMenuItem_Click" Text="Aerial Mode"/>

<shell:ApplicationBarMenuItem
 Click="ApplicationBarMenuItem_Click_1" Text="Road Mode"/>
```

15. Open your `MainPage.xaml.cs` file and you will find the two click event functions created automatically: `ApplicationBarMenuItem_Click` and `ApplicationBarMenuItem_Click_1`.

16. As the first menu item is for Aerial Mode, we set the map mode to Aerial Mode by using the following code in the `ApplicationBarMenuItem_Click` function:

```
private void ApplicationBarMenuItem_Click(object sender,
EventArgs e)
    {
        myMap.Mode = new AerialMode();
    }
```

17. Note the `myMap` variable was assigned to the **Map** control in step 8.

18. Similarly we do the same for the `ApplicationBarMenuItem_Click_1` function, however here we set the mode to Road by using the following code:

```
private void ApplicationBarMenuItem_Click_1(object sender,
EventArgs e)
    {
        myMap.Mode = newRoadMode();
    }
```

19. Run the application in the emulator and click on the three dots you see on the lower right-hand side of your application footer. This invokes the Application Bar and your app screen should like the following screenshot:

20. Select the **aerial mode** menu item and see your map change to Aerial Mode in real-time. You can switch back to Road Mode by selecting the **road mode** menu item again.

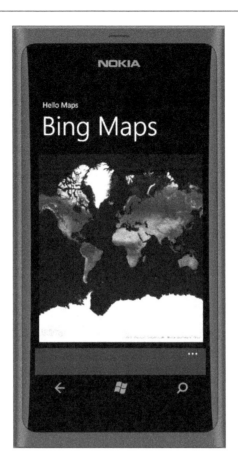

You can find this example project in the code files for the book under `Chapter 3`, titled `HelloMaps`.

Using pushpins with maps

We have seen how to change map modes, however just a simple map without any focus does not make much sense, does it? So we move further and modify the `HelloMaps` example by using the Windows Phone Location Service to add a pushpin to the map – signifying the user's detected location.

The Pushpin class is part of the Microsoft.Phone.Controls.Maps namespace, with location as one of the properties. So let's use this property in our code and render a simple pushpin:

1.   We start by creating a new project titled HelloMaps-Pushpin.

2.   From our HelloMaps example, reintegrate the same UI, maps, and text labels, and from our Hello Location example, import the TextBlock named statusText. Your UI should now look like the following screenshot:

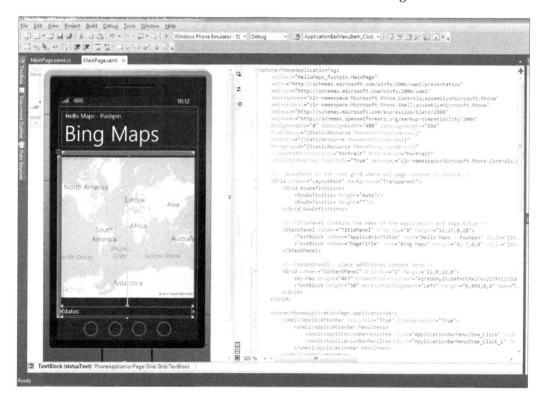

3.   Open MainPage.xaml.cs and copy over the location variable and methods from the Hello Location example. Add a variable in the global scope called zoomLevel that controls your map's zoom level.

```
GeoCoordinateWatcher locationManager;
double zoomLevel = 10.00;
```

4. Now in your `MainPage()` constructor copy over the location manager code from the Hello Location example, and for your map, set `ZoomBarVisibility` to `Visible`. This property is from the `Map` class that allows the zoom in/zoom out control to be visible on the map. The following is your constructor code:

```
public MainPage()
{
  InitializeComponent();
  locationManager = new
  GeoCoordinateWatcher(GeoPositionAccuracy.High);

  locationManager.StatusChanged += new
    EventHandler<GeoPositionStatusChangedEventArgs>
    (locationManager_getStatus);

  locationManager.PositionChanged += new
    EventHandler<GeoPositionChangedEventArgs<GeoCoordinate>>
    (locationManager_getPosition);

  myMap.ZoomBarVisibility = Visibility.Visible;
  locationManager.Start();
}
```

5. The `StatusChanged` event handler `locationManager_getStatus` remains similar to the `Hello Location` example, however the `PositionChanged` event handler undergoes a few changes by adding a new pushpin at the detected location.

6. We begin the `PositionChanged` event handler function by creating a new pushpin named `myPin`. The `Location` property of the `Pushpin` class is then used to transfer the hardware's detected location to the pushpin by the following lines of code:

```
void locationManager_getPosition(object sender,
 GeoPositionChangedEventArgs<GeoCoordinate> newLoc)
{
  Pushpin myPin = new Pushpin();
  myPin.Location = new
    GeoCoordinate(newLoc.Position.Location.Latitude,
    newLoc.Position.Location.Longitude);
```

7. Now we add this pushpin to the map by using the `Children` collection of the `Map` class as:

```
myMap.Children.Add(myPin);
```

8. Lastly, we change the map's current view to the detected location to focus the map at that geocoordinate and specify a zoom level.

```
myMap.SetView(new GeoCoordinate(newLoc.Position.Location.
Latitude,newLoc.Position.Location.Longitude), zoomLevel);
```

Don't forget to import the following `Location` and `Maps` namespaces in your C# code:

```
using Microsoft.Phone.Controls;
using Microsoft.Phone.Controls.Maps;
using System.Device.Location;
```

9. Running the application in the emulator produces the following result:

10. Now open up the **Location** simulator and select a few locations around **Paris**. Do it one at a time and see the real-time pushpin magic!!

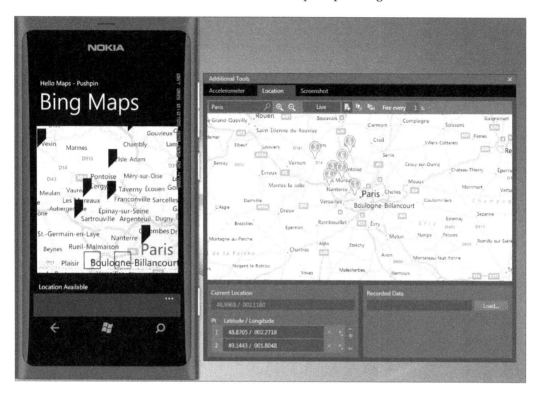

You can find this example project in the code files for the book under Chapter 3, titled HelloMaps-Pushpin.

Custom map pushpins

We created our own maps application and added a pushpin. Great! But does it look great? To be honest – no, the black pushpin icon is not fancy. In fact the pushpins in the **Location** simulator are better! (We hope Microsoft guys are reading this line.) We can, however, use the following code to add some content to the pushpin, but it still does not give us the "wow" look:

```
myPin.Content =  newLoc.Position.Location.Latitude.ToString() +
  ", " +newLoc.Position.Location.Longitude.ToString();
```

Thankfully the Windows Phone Bing Maps Silverlight Control provides the ability to use our own icons for the pushpin. There are two ways to use custom map pushpins:

- Using an image as the pushpin
- Using your own pushpin style (in XAML)

 The guys at `http://365psd.com/` have some excellent and free map pushpin icons. You can find a few at `http://365psd.com/?s=map`. We use the one from Dennis Covent: `http://365psd.com/day/2-302/` as the custom icon for our pushpin.

Using an image as the pushpin

Let us use the icon mentioned previously as an image for our pushpins:

1. Open the `HelloMaps-Pushpin` example and navigate to the `MainPage.xaml.cs` file.

2. Declare an object of type `MapLayer` in the global namespace.

   ```
   MapLayer myMapLayer;
   ```

3. In the `MainPage()` constructor initialize the `myMapLayer` object and add it to the map as:

   ```
   myMapLayer = new MapLayer();
   myMap.Children.Add(myMapLayer);
   ```

4. In your `locationManager_getPosition` function add the following lines of code and comment out the rest:

   ```
   void locationManager_getPosition(object sender,
    GeoPositionChangedEventArgs<GeoCoordinate> newLoc)
   {

   // Custom PushPin
     Image pushpinImage = new Image();
     pushpinImage.Source = new
       System.Windows.Media.Imaging.BitmapImage
       (newUri("myPushPin.png", UriKind.Relative));

     pushpinImage.Opacity = 0.7;
     pushpinImage.Stretch = System.Windows.Media.Stretch.None;
     PositionOrigin position = PositionOrigin.Center;
   ```

```
myMapLayer.AddChild(pushpinImage,
  new GeoCoordinate(newLoc.Position.Location.Latitude,
  newLoc.Position.Location.Longitude), position);

// End of Custom PushPin
  myMap.SetView(new GeoCoordinate
  (newLoc.Position.Location.Latitude,
  newLoc.Position.Location.Longitude), zoomLevel);
}
```

5. Do not forget to add the `myPushPin.png` image to your project.

6. Note the highlighted code in step 4. It adds `pushpinImage`to the `myMapLayer` object at the location detected, and adds our pushpin icon in at the center of the view.

7. Run the application now to see the custom pushpin icons in action as shown in the following screenshot:

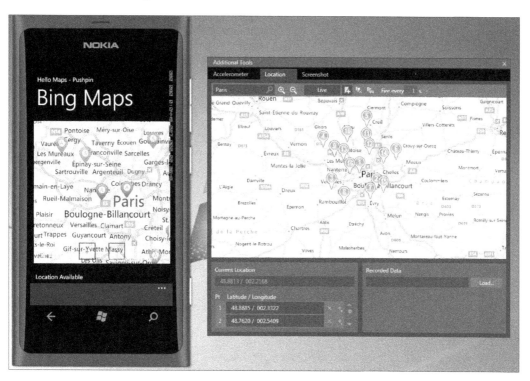

Using your own pushpin style

We saw how to use the image as a layer instead of a pushpin. Some developers would not want to work with a pushpin in this way. The `Image` and `Pushpin` classes are quite different in their own sense, each having their own properties, methods, constructors, and events. So using a layer is not always equal to a pushpin implementation. So using a layer is not always equal to a pushpin implementation.

In such cases we define a new XAML style in `App.xaml`, the main class that calls `MainPage.xaml` within the `<Application.Resources></Application.Resources>` tags:

1. Open your project `HelloMaps-Pushpin`. Navigate to the `App.xaml` file and add the following style markup within the `<Application.Resources></Application.Resources>` tags:

```
<Style TargetType="m:Pushpin" x:Key="myPushpinStyle">
  <Setter Property="Template">
    <Setter.Value>
      <ControlTemplate TargetType="m:Pushpin">
        <Grid x:Name="ContentGrid">
          <Image Source="myPushPin.png" Stretch="None"/>
        </Grid>
      </ControlTemplate>
    </Setter.Value>
  </Setter>
</Style>
```

2. Now in your `MainPage.xaml.cs` file uncomment the default pushpin code that we commented earlier.

```
// Standard Pushpin

myPin.Content = newLoc.Position.Location.Latitude.ToString()
  + ", " +newLoc.Position.Location.Longitude.ToString();

myPin.Style =
  (Style)(Application.Current.Resources["myPushpinStyle"]);

myPin.Location = newGeoCoordinate
  (newLoc.Position.Location.Latitude,
  newLoc.Position.Location.Longitude);
myMap.Children.Add(myPin);

// End of Standard Pushpin
```

3. With the addition of the code highlighted in the previous step, here we are using the style we defined in `App.xaml` and assigning it to our pushpin object.

4. Running the app will result in an almost similar icon display as shown earlier, the only difference being the `Opacity` parameter set previously, which we haven't put in our style.

Handling pushpin events

Handling pushpin events is fairly simple. For example, to handle a simple mouse left-click event we use the `MouseButtonEventHandler` event handler as:

```
myPin.MouseLeftButtonUp += new
  MouseButtonEventHandler(myPin_MouseLeftButtonUp);
```

Here `myPin_MouseLeftButtonUp` is our function that will execute when the event triggers. We declare this as a simple function that shows a message box alert.

```
void myPin_MouseLeftButtonUp(object sender,
  MouseButtonEventArgs e)
{
  Pushpin localPushPin = new Pushpin();
  localPushPin = (Pushpin) sender;

  MessageBox.Show("You are Here : " +
    localPushPin.Location.Latitude + "," +
    localPushPin.Location.Longitude);
}
```

The following screenshot shows how it will look in the emulator:

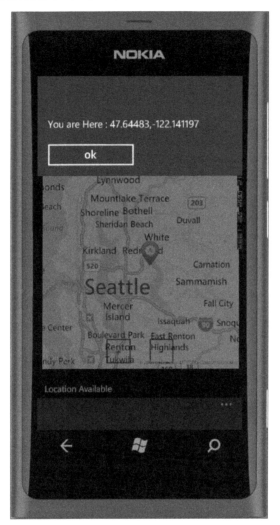

Working with Bing Maps geocoding and reverse geocoding services

The Bing Maps REST Services API provides API end points for forward geocoding (or just simple geocoding) as well as reverse geocoding. Static Maps API, Routing and Traffic APIs are supported as well. Refer to the following MSDN documentation for a complete look at the APIs:

http://msdn.microsoft.com/en-us/library/ff701722.aspx

In our previous example, we showed an alert when a user clicked or touched on a pushpin. The content of the alert was geocodes, however to make the app more informational and useful, we could use the reverse geocoding API from Bing Maps, and convert the geocodes to meaningful addresses. Here's how:

1. We use the **Find a Location by Point** API endpoint from the Bing Maps REST Service at:

   ```
   http://msdn.microsoft.com/en-us/library/ff701710.aspx
   ```

2. Import the following XML namespaces in your project so that we can parse the API response:

   ```
   using System.Xml;
   using System.Xml.Linq;
   ```

3. In your global class namespace, create a new variable of type `WebClient`, which will be used to send the API request.

   ```
   WebClient myWebClient;
   ```

4. Next, in your `MainPage()` constructor, initialize the `myWebClient` variable as:

   ```
   myWebClient = new WebClient();
   ```

5. In our `myPin_MouseLeftButtonUp` event function, define a function callback for the `myWebClient` object and name it `myWebClient_DownloadStringCompleted`.

6. Now create a `Uri` object that contains the API link for the Bing Maps reverse geocoding API endpoint and initiate the API request. Your code should now look as follows:

   ```
   void myPin_MouseLeftButtonUp(object sender,
    MouseButtonEventArgs e)
   {
     Pushpin localPushPin = new Pushpin();
     localPushPin = (Pushpin) sender;
     myWebClient.DownloadStringCompleted +=
      new DownloadStringCompletedEventHandler
      (myWebClient_DownloadStringCompleted);
     Uri uri = new Uri
      ("http://dev.virtualearth.net/REST/v1/Locations/" +
      localPushPin.Location.Latitude + ","
      +localPushPin.Location.Longitude+
      "?o=xml&key=xxxxxxxxxxxxxxx");
     myWebClient.DownloadStringAsync(uri);
   }
   ```

7. Note that xxxxxxxxxxxxxxx is your Bing Maps key that we obtained from the Bing Maps App Portal.

8. As the web client requests get completed, our predefined callback function `myWebClient_DownloadStringCompleted` is fired, where we parse the XML response, find the right tag, and display an alert to the user.

```
private void myWebClient_DownloadStringCompleted(object sender,
 DownloadStringCompletedEventArgs e)
{

  XElement xml = XElement.Parse(e.Result);
  XNamespace xmlNameSpace =
    "http://schemas.microsoft.com/search/local/ws/rest/v1";

  MessageBox.Show("You are Here : " +
    xml.Descendants(xmlNameSpace + "Name").First().Value);
}
```

9. We use the `XElement.Parse()` method to parse the XML response from the Bing Maps API. Note the use of the `XNamespace` object to search through the XML response. The following screenshot shows a sample response:

10. We used the `<Name>` tag from the response to display the address to the user.

11. Running the app in the emulator produces the following result:

You can find this example project in the code files for the book under `Chapter 3`, titled `HelloMaps-Pushpin`.

Launchers and Choosers – An Overview

Launchers and **Choosers** are some other exceptional fundamental concepts in Windows Phone 7.5. They allow application developers to access the address book, web browsers, maps, messaging, and camera support without writing much code. The idea here is not to import tons of libraries and reuse the same functionality, but to pass control to the right application (system application) to get the job done and come back to the main application with the result.

Launchers are a set of API tasks that allow the user to navigate to other parts of the Windows Phone experience to accomplish a certain goal. However Launchers return no control back to the user or the calling program. Some examples of Launchers are e-mail, marketplace, SMS, web browser, media player, and the Bing Maps task. A complete list of available Launchers is shown in the following table:

Launcher name	Launcher description
BingMapsDirectionsTask	Used for displaying directions from a starting location or to an end location.
BingMapsTask	Launches the Bing Maps application. This could be used to fire predefined searches from within our app.
ConnectionSettingsTask	Used to adjust the device's network connection settings.
EmailComposeTask	Used to send e-mail from your application.
MarketplaceDetailTask	Loads the Marketplace details page for a specified application.
MarketplaceHubTask	Launches the Marketplace with the specified hub name. For example, *music* will launch the Marketplace with applications that cater to the music category.
MarketplaceReviewTask	Loads the Marketplace with the current application's review page.
MarketplaceSearchTask	Loads the Marketplace and populates it with the search results for the specified search keyword.
MediaPlayerLauncher	Launches the Media player.
PhoneCallTask	Allows the user to make a phone call from our application.
SearchTask	Performs a web search.
ShareLinkTask	Enables the user to share a link on social network(s).
ShareStatusTask	Enables the user to share his status on social network(s).
SmsComposeTask	Sends an SMS message from our application.
WebBrowserTask	Launches the web browser with the specified URL.

Choosers are similar to Launchers, with the exception that Choosers return some data back to the calling application. Some examples would be contact selection, photo selection, or the device camera, where the application expects a selection result to do further processing.

A list of Choosers available in Windows Phone 7.5 is shown in the following table:

Chooser name	Chooser description
AddressChooserTask	Launches the address book and allows the user to choose a contact.
CameraCaptureTask	Captures an image from the camera and returns it to our application.
EmailAddressChooserTask	Launches the address book and allows the user to choose a contact. The contact's e-mail field is returned to the application.
GameInviteTask	Invite players to a multiplayer Xbox LIVE game.
PhoneNumberChooserTask	Launches the address book and allows the user to choose a contact. The contact's phone number is returned to the application.
PhotoChooserTask	Selects an existing photo from the phone.
SaveContactTask	Saves a contact from your application using the Contacts application.
SaveEmailAddressTask	Saves an e-mail address from your application using the Contacts application.
SavePhoneNumberTask	Saves a phone number from your application using the Contacts application.
SaveRingtoneTask	Saves an audio file as a ringtone.

 To use Launchers or Choosers, your application must import the Microsoft.Phone.Tasks namespace. To read more about Launchers see the MSDN documentation at http://msdn.microsoft.com/en-us/library/ff769550%28v=vs.92%29.aspx, and for Choosers see the MSDN documentation at http://msdn.microsoft.com/en-us/library/ff769543%28v=vs.92%29.aspx.

Using directions with Bing Maps directions task

We got acquainted with Launchers in our previous topic. Let us now look at `BingMapsDirectionsTask`, and use it to provide driving directions from within our application:

1. Create a copy of our `HelloMaps-Pushpin` project and rename it `HelloMaps-Directions`.

2. Open your `MainPage.xaml.cs` file and import the `Microsoft.Phone.Tasks` namespace into your project.

    ```
    using Microsoft.Phone.Tasks;
    ```

3. Assuming the maps center as **Redmond**, we want to show driving directions to the nearby **Mercer Island** as depicted in the following screenshot:

4. We begin by defining a variable `myDrivingDirection` of type `BingMapsDirectionsTask` as:

```
BingMapsDirectionsTask myDrivingDirection;
```

5. In our `MainPage()` constructor, we define the start and end points of our route. The start being some location near **Redmond** and end being **Mercer Island**.

```
// Show driving directions to Mercer Island
// Use "null" as the starting location to use your current
// location as the starting point.

myDrivingDirection = new BingMapsDirectionsTask();
myDrivingDirection.Start = new LabeledMapLocation
  ("My Location", newGeoCoordinate(47.6601, -122.13333));
myDrivingDirection.End = new LabeledMapLocation
  ("Mercer Island", null);
// End of driving directions
```

6. We added a HyperlinkButton near the footer (as shown in the previous screenshot), that will be used to fire the `start()` method of the `BingMapsDirectionsTask` instance.

```
private void hyperlinkButton1_Click(object sender,
  RoutedEventArgs e)
{
  myDrivingDirection.Show();
}
```

7. Run the application now and click on the **Show Directions** hyperlink button. You should see the following output (tested on our Nokia Lumia 800):

Pretty simple, huh? It is that easy to incorporate directions in your apps – no more extensive SDKs, libraries, and tons of code to import within your app. In pure Windows folklore we would say "Plug and Play" directions. You can find this example project in the code files for the book under `Chapter 3`, titled `HelloMaps-Directions`.

Performing local searches with BingMapsTask

The `BingMapsTask` is similar to the `BingMapsDirectionsTask` Launcher, except for the difference that `BingMapsTask` launches the Bing Maps app from the Windows Phone, and can allow it to be pre-populated with a search keyword or mark locations on the map.

We can modify the previous example to use `BingMapsTask` and populate a search result for `Pizza` when the hyperlink button **Search for Pizza** is clicked or touched:

1. Create a copy of our `HelloMaps-Pushpin` project and rename it `HelloMaps-Search`.

2. Import the `Microsoft.Phone.Tasks` namespace.

3. Declare an instance of `BingMapsTask` in your main class as:

   ```
   BingMapsTask myBingMapsTask;
   ```

4. In the `MainPage()` constructor, we instantiate `myBingMapsTask`, center it to a position near **Redmond**, and finally define the search term as `Pizza` using the following lines of code:

   ```
   // Show Bing Maps and search for Pizza
   myBingMapsTask = new BingMapsTask();
   myBingMapsTask.Center = new GeoCoordinate
   (47.6601, -122.13333);
   myBingMapsTask.SearchTerm = "Pizza";

   // End of  Bing Maps
   ```

5. Add the `Click()` method of `hyperlinkButton1` as:

   ```
   private void hyperlinkButton1_Click(object sender,
    RoutedEventArgs e)
   {
     myBingMapsTask.Show();
   }
   ```

6. Running the app produces the following result:

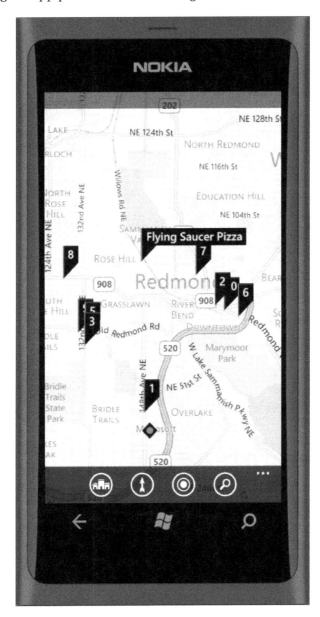

Memory allocated for a `BingMapsTask` does not count towards the total memory usage of your application. So try to use `BingMapsTask` instead of the Bing Maps Silverlight Control in your memory constraint devices/applications.

You can find this example project in the code files for the book under `Chapter 3`, titled `HelloMaps-Search`.

Summary

In this chapter we learnt how to use Bing Maps and its various controls in our Windows Phone applications.

Specifically we covered an overview of map geometry – analysis of how maps work – using the Bing Maps Silverlight control, working with pushpins and custom pushpins, handling pushpin events, working with the Bing Maps geocoding service, and using Bing Maps Launchers (`BingMapsDirectionsTask` and `BingMapsTask`) in our Windows Phone applications.

In the next chapter we will create a real-world Windows Phone application that leverages `Eventful.com` events and location, and maps them into the user experience. So keep reading.

4
Events App - PacktEvents

Entertainment and music applications are now customary additions available with all smartphones today. On the Nokia Lumia 800 Windows Phone 7.5 device, we have the **Zune music player** that allows us to listen to music, watch videos, and subscribe to podcasts and radio as well. Another interesting app that was recently launched in the Windows Marketplace is the **Nokia music app**, which presents a good UI to listen to music, as well as listing gigs (events) happening nearby.

An events app is a good entertainment companion for your Windows Phone. By using the events application, users can browse for nearby gigs, get to know more about their favorite artists, and find events happening at their favorite venue.

Eventful.com is the leading events and entertainment service that provides real-time events information to millions of users, the killer feature being **Demand it!** – a service that empowers fans to get their favorite artists/performers to come to their town and perform.

In this chapter, we will learn how to build a complete events app from scratch using the Eventful.com API. The application name will be PacktEvents.

This chapter covers:

- Exploring the Eventful.com API
- Extending the Hello Location example for showing nearby events
- Filtering events by categories
- Plotting events on Bing Maps
- Building the PacktEvents app using Panorama control

Exploring the Eventful.com API

`Eventful.com` provides an extensive concerts and events API via `api.eventful.com`, which allows third-party developers to:

- Integrate the rich and unique events information into their applications
- Create and edit new events
- Add images and comments
- Create, edit, or modify a venue
- Search for venues and events
- Get user information: User-created events, venues, and events attended by a user
- Add and edit artist information
- Get a list of event categories
- Search for demands and get the details of a demand

The demand feature is a unique concept from Eventful, which can be used by consumers to demand that their favorite artists come to their cities and perform a gig.

The events content is tagged in the following ways:

- Events are tied to a location with latitude and longitude and mapped to a venue(s) in a city
- Events are tied to artists
- Events are categorized into specific pre-defined categories, such as concerts, jazz, dance, and so on
- Event details include start date, end date, time of event, ticket price, and so on
- Events can be searched by keywords and/or location
- Events can also be retrieved based on popularity

Similarly venues and artists have corresponding API endpoints. Find a complete list of API endpoints at `http://api.eventful.com/docs`. We will explain the various endpoints as we continue building our app.

Extending the Hello Location example for showing nearby events

In *Chapter 2, Using Location in Windows Phone 7.5*, we saw a simple location example titled "Hello Location" that showed our location information. We will extend this to build a location-enabled events app using the Eventful API.

The following are essential before we start building our location-enabled events app:

- An API key is required. Register for one at `http://api.eventful.com/signup`.

- Hands-on with XML parsing using `XElement`. See `XElement.parse` example in *Chapter 3, Using Maps in your Windows Phone App*.

We will use the simple Windows Phone application template to create a new sample application titled `Hello Events`, and add a new page to it; so let's begin:

1. Open the **Microsoft Visual Studio 2010 Express for Windows Phone** IDE, and create a new project by selecting **File | New Project**. Select the **Windows Phone Application** template within the **Visual C#** option; **Name** it as `HelloEvents`.

2. Copy the code and UI from our `Hello Location` example within the `MainPage.xaml` and `MainPage.xaml.cs` files that mimic the `Hello Location` app.

3. Next, right-click on your project name in **Solution Explorer** and select **Add | New Item**, as shown in the following screenshot:

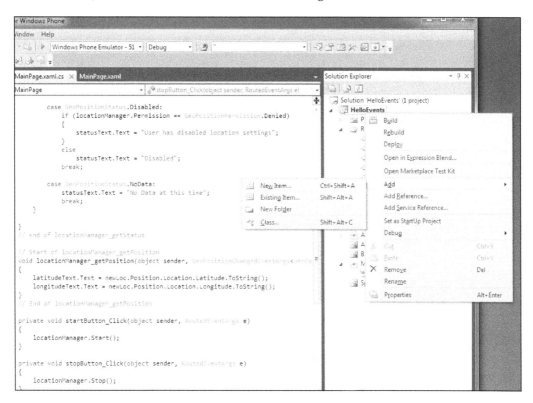

4. From the **Add New Item** pop up page select the **Windows Phone Portrait Page** option. **Name** the page EventPage.xaml, as shown in the following screenshot:

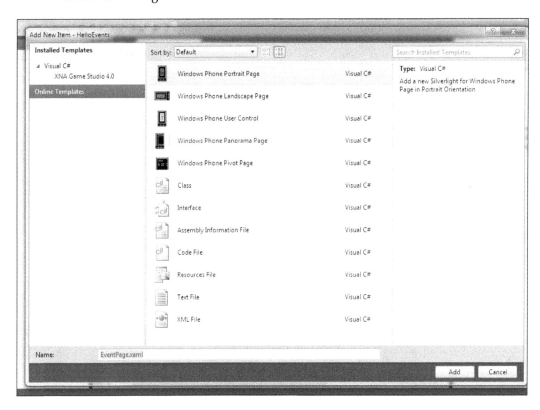

5. Now in your MainPage.xaml, add a new button titled Show Events. This button will fire an event that will load the EventPage.xaml page and load ten nearby events from the Eventful API, by passing in the location values obtained from the GeoCoordinateWatcher object.

6. Define the Click handler for your Show Events button in the MainPage.xaml file as:

```
<Button Content="Show Events" Height="72"
HorizontalAlignment="Left" Margin="-4,270,0,0" Name="button1"
VerticalAlignment="Top" Width="207" Click="showEvents_Click" />
```

7. Now let us define the showEvents_Click() event handler function. We use the NavigationService class to navigate across the various pages in our application. As we want to pass in the latitude and longitude pair to our Events Page, we send it as a query string to the NavigationService. Navigate method as:

```
Private void showEvents_Click(objectsender,RoutedEventArgs e)
{
  NavigationService.Navigate(
   new Uri("/EventPage.xaml?latitude=" + latitudeText.Text +
   "&longitude="+longitudeText.Text, UriKind.Relative)
   );
}
```

8. Now let's start writing some code to fetch the nearby events from the Eventful API, and display the details on the events page of our application. We begin by declaring a variable of type `WebClient` and a string variable to store our Eventful API key in our `EventPage` class declaration in the `EventPage.xaml.cs` file.

```
public partial class EventPage :PhoneApplicationPage
{
  WebClient myWebClient;
  String apiKey = "xxxxxxxxxxxxx"; // Get your own key from
  //eventful.com

public EventPage()
{
    InitializeComponent();
```

9. As we will be using the XML API from `Eventful.com`, don't forget to include the `System.Xml` and `System.Xml.Linq` namespaces. For debugging we added the `System.Diagnostics` namespace as well. You may need to **Add Reference** to the libraries from the **Solution Explorer | References** tab.

```
using System.Xml;
using System.Xml.Linq;
using System.Diagnostics;
```

10. Next, initialize the `WebClient` variable in the `EventPage()` constructor as:

```
myWebClient = new WebClient();
```

11. We use the `OnNavigatedTo` overridable method of the `PhoneApplicationPage` class to notify our `EventPage` class that the page *has been navigated to* (the page has been visited or browsed). Here is where we catch the passed location query by using the `NavigationContext` class's `QueryString` method.

12. We then pass on the latitude and longitude values to the `Eventful.com` API via the `myWebClient` variable and initiate the web request, the callback function being `myWebClient_DownloadStringCompleted`.

```
Protected override void
 OnNavigatedTo(System.Windows.Navigation.NavigationEventArgs e)
{
  base.OnNavigatedTo(e);
```

```
       string latitude= NavigationContext.QueryString["latitude"];
       string longitude= NavigationContext.QueryString["longitude"];

     // Load Events from Eventful.com API
       myWebClient.DownloadStringCompleted += new
       DownloadStringCompletedEventHandler
       (myWebClient_DownloadStringCompleted);

       Uri uri = new Uri
     ("http://api.eventful.com/rest/events/search?keywords=concerts&
      location=" + latitude + "," + longitude +
      "&app_key="+apiKey+"&within=10");

       myWebClient.DownloadStringAsync(uri);

     // End of Eventful API call.
     }
```

13. To display the nearby events (we are searching for nearby concerts), we added a `ListBox` control to the `EventPage.xaml` file, as well as a `ProgressBar` control (the awesome loading animation you see in almost all Windows Phone 7.5 apps), and enable its animation activity by setting the `IsIndeterminate` property to `true` as shown in the following code:

```
<ProgressBar Name="loadingBar" Margin="0,251,0,263"
 IsIndeterminate="true">
</ProgressBar>
<ListBox Height="595" HorizontalAlignment="Left"
 Margin="2,6,0,0" Name="myEventsList" VerticalAlignment="Top"
 Width="448">
</ListBox>
```

14. Now when the API request completes downloading the response, the `myWebClient_DownloadStringCompleted` method parses the XML and appends the events titles to the `ListBox` control we added in the `EventPage.xaml` file. We also set the `ProgressBar` control to inactive and collapse it. We use the `List` class from `System.Collections.Generic` and create a list of string objects that represent the event name from the XML response. When we are done collecting the event names in the list object, we assign the list object as the source to our ListBox.

```
private void myWebClient_DownloadStringCompleted(object sender,
 DownloadStringCompletedEventArgs e)
{
   XElement xml = XElement.Parse(e.Result);
   // Best practice for pausing a ProgressBar loading animation.
```

```
    loadingBar.IsIndeterminate = false;
    loadingBar.Visibility = Visibility.Collapsed;

    List<string>myListItem = newList<string>();
    IEnumerable<XElement> elements = xml.Descendants("event");

    foreach (XElement element in elements)
    {
      myListItem.Add(element.Element("title").Value);
    }
    myEventsList.ItemsSource = myListItem;
}
```

15. Running the application in the emulator produces the following screenshot:

16. Clicking on the **Show Events** button produces the following screenshot:

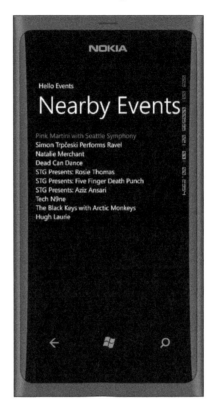

For real-world results, run it on your Nokia Lumia 800 or any other Windows Phone 7.5 device, to find nearby events! Notice the back button on the Events Page; this will take you back to the **Your Location** page automatically. You can also customize the back button behavior, by changing the `BackStack` property in the `NavigationService` class. Refer to the *Back Stack* page on MSDN at `http://msdn.microsoft.com/en-us/library/hh394012(v=vs.92).aspx`.

You can find this example project in the code files for the book under `Chapter 4,` titled `HelloEvents`.

Filtering events by categories

`Eventful.com` has a rich set of categories that cover the breadth of events happening around the globe; from music to business events, varied types of events are available. There may be users who are interested only in concert events, while another group of users prefer sports events. Customization that suits the end user's taste is key to an app's success.

The following table shows all categories of events supported by the Eventful API:

Category ID	Category name
music	Concerts & Tour Dates
conference	Conferences & Tradeshows
learning_education	Education
family_fun_kids	Kids & Family
festivals_parades	Festivals
movies_film	Film
food	Food & Wine
fundraisers	Fundraising & charity
art	Art Galleries & Exhibits
support	Health & Wellness
books	Library & Books
attractions	Museums & Attractions
community	Neighborhood
business	Business & Networking
singles_social	Nightlife & Singles
schools_alumni	University & Alumni
clubs_association	Organizations & Meetups
outdoors_recreation	Outdoors & Recreation
performing_arts	Performing Arts
animals	Pets
politics_activisim	Politics & Activism
sales	Sales & Retail
science	Science
religion_spirituality	Religion & Spirituality
sports	Sports
technology	Technology
other	Other and Miscellaneous

 Most of the API calls work by using the category ID. The category name is for display purposes; avoid it wherever possible. The category ID is preferred as it is all lowercase, clean, and has *no special character-based* keyword.

We extend the HelloEvents example we saw previously, and use the Eventful category API to filter events:

1. Create a new **Silverlight for Windows Phone** project and **Name** it HelloEvents-Categories.

2. Copy the XAML and C# code from the MainPage.xaml and MainPage.xaml.cs files of the HelloEvents example. However, on the home screen, change the text of the Show Events button to List Categories, as we will now be showing a list of event categories and then the actual events, based on the category selection.

3. Also change the click event method name to showCategories_Click, as shown in the following XAML code for the new List Categories button:

```
<Button Content="List Categories" Height="72"
 HorizontalAlignment="Left" Margin="-4,270,0,0" Name="button1"
 VerticalAlignment="Top" Width="231"
 Click="showCategories_Click" />
```

4. Now on the Click event, we will not be showing the Events Page as we did earlier; instead, we will create a new **Windows Phone Portrait Page** (CategoryPage.xaml) and use that as the second screen.

```
private void showCategories_Click(object sender,
 RoutedEventArgs e)
{
  NavigationService.Navigate(
   new Uri("/CategoryPage.xaml?latitude=" + latitudeText.Text +
   "&longitude=" + longitudeText.Text, UriKind.Relative)
   );
}
```

5. Our Category Page is a simple page that will show the event categories fetched from the Eventful.com API. Add the ProgressBar and ListBox control to your CategoryPage.xaml file to make it look like the following screenshot:

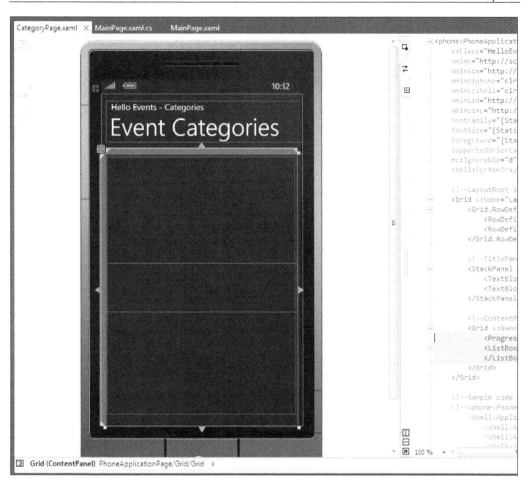

6. In our `CategoryPage.xaml.cs` file, we add the variables similar to our `HelloEvents` example, however, now we add two more `List` variables of type string – one to hold the **category ID** and another to hold the **category name**.

```
public partial class CategoryPage :PhoneApplicationPage
{
  WebClient myWebClient;
  String apiKey = "xxxxxxxxxxx";  // Get your own key from
  //Eventful

  List<string> myCategoryId;
  List<string> myCategoryName;
  string latitude;
  string longitude;
```

7. Note, we will not be using the latitude and longitude obtained from the MainPage (the `MainPage.xaml.cs` file). However, we need these variables to pass to our third page – `EventPage.xaml`.

8. In our `CategoryPage()` constructor, we initialize the following variables:

```
myWebClient = new WebClient();
myCategoryName = new List<string>();
myCategoryId = new List<string>();
```

9. Now in our navigation service's `OnNavigatedTo` method, we store the latitude and longitude obtained from the MainPage (the `MainPage.xaml.cs` file) and call the `Eventful.com` API to get a list of all categories.

```
Protected override void
 OnNavigatedTo(System.Windows.Navigation.NavigationEventArgs e)
{
  base.OnNavigatedTo(e);

  latitude = NavigationContext.QueryString["latitude"];
  longitude = NavigationContext.QueryString["longitude"];

  // Load Event Categories from Eventful.com API
  myWebClient.DownloadStringCompleted += new
   DownloadStringCompletedEventHandler
   (myWebClient_DownloadStringCompleted);

  Uri uri = new Uri
   ("http://api.evdb.com/rest/categories/list?app_key="
   + apiKey);

  myWebClient.DownloadStringAsync(uri);
  // End of Eventful API call.
}
```

10. We modify the `myWebClient_DownloadStringCompleted` method and change the name of the XML tags to be parsed, as well as some string replacement to enhance the display.

```
private void myWebClient_DownloadStringCompleted(object sender,
 DownloadStringCompletedEventArgs e)
{
  XElement xml = XElement.Parse(e.Result);
  loadingBar.IsIndeterminate = false;
  loadingBar.Visibility = Visibility.Collapsed; ;

  IEnumerable<XElement> elements = xml.Descendants("category");
```

```
foreach (XElement element in elements)
{
  String categoryName = element.Element("name").Value.Replace
    ("&amp;", "&");
  String categoryId = element.Element("id").Value;
  myCategoryId.Add(categoryId);
  myCategoryName.Add(categoryName);
}

myCategoriesList.ItemsSource = myCategoryName;
}
```

11. Notice how we added the category ID and category name to different `List` variables. We did this purposely, as the index of both of the list items will be same, so mapping the category name to category ID will be easier. As mentioned earlier, the `Eventful.com` API works well with the category ID and not category name, as the former is cleaner text.

12. We use the `SelectionChanged` attribute of the `ListBox` control to define the method that will be fired when the user selects any item from the ListBox. This is done on the XAML side in our `CategoryPage.xaml` as:

```
<ListBox Height="595" HorizontalAlignment="Left"
 Margin="2,6,0,0" Name="myCategoriesList"
 VerticalAlignment="Top" Width="448"
 SelectionChanged="showEvents">
```

13. The `showEvents` method is where the third page of the application is called, and the latitude/longitude pair along with the event category selected is passed as a query string to the third XAML page, which is `EventPage.xaml`.

```
private void showEvents(object sender,
 SelectionChangedEventArgs e)
{
  String selectedCategoryId =
   myCategoryId[myCategoriesList.SelectedIndex];

  NavigationService.Navigate(new
   Uri("/EventPage.xaml?latitude=" + latitude + "&longitude=" +
   longitude + "&categoryId=" + selectedCategoryId,
   UriKind.Relative)
   );
}
```

14. Notice the highlighted code in the previous step, where we are getting the category ID corresponding to the category Name selected from the list box. As the `List<string>` can be accessed by **index**, we add the appropriate values to the category ID list and category name list (`myCategoryId` and `myCategoryName`) and access it as we need. Alternatively we could have chosen to use a multi-dimensional array.

15. Our `EventPage.xaml.cs` remains mostly the same as before, except for the addition of the category ID in the `Eventful.com` API to fetch nearby events. Note, the API URL changes a bit too, as shown in the following lines of code:

```
protected override void
 OnNavigatedTo(System.Windows.Navigation.NavigationEventArgs e)
{
  base.OnNavigatedTo(e);
  string latitude = NavigationContext.QueryString["latitude"];
  string longitude =
   NavigationContext.QueryString["longitude"];
  stringcategoryId =
   NavigationContext.QueryString["categoryId"];
  // Load Events from Eventful.com API

  myWebClient.DownloadStringCompleted +=
   new DownloadStringCompletedEventHandler
   (myWebClient_DownloadStringCompleted);

  Uri uri = new
  Uri("http://api.eventful.com/rest/events/search?category=" +
   categoryId + "&location=" + latitude + "," + longitude +
   "&app_key=" + apiKey + "&within=10");

  myWebClient.DownloadStringAsync(uri);

  // End of Eventful API call.
}
```

16. It's emulator time now! Run the application on the emulator; you should get the following screenshot:

17. Clicking on the **List Categories** button loads `CategoryPage.xaml` as shown in the following screenshot:

18. Select any event category; let's say **Festivals**, which loads `EventPage.xaml` with events for the selected category, as shown in the following screenshot:

Observe how the back button works seamlessly; play around with the location and event categories to see different events worldwide.

You can find this example project in the code files for the book under `Chapter 4`, titled `HelloEvents-Categories`.

Plotting events on Bing Maps

In *Chapter 3, Using Maps in your Windows Phone App*, we saw how to use Bing Maps and pushpins within our apps. Now, let us use that knowledge to incorporate maps within our "Hello Events" franchise:

1. Create a new **Silverlight for Windows Phone** project and **Name** it
   `HelloEvents-Maps`.

2. Copy the code and UI from our previous `HelloEvents-Categories`
   example. We will make some changes in the `EventPage.xaml` and
   `EventPage.xaml.cs` files to show maps and events plotted on the maps.

3. Add a button and a map control to your `EventPage.xaml` file just below the
   `ListBox` control. Your `ContentPanel` grid should now contain the following
   lines of code:

   ```
   <Grid x:Name="ContentPanel" Grid.Row="1" Margin="12,0,12,30">
     <ProgressBar Name="loadingBar" Margin="0,251,0,263"
     IsIndeterminate="true"></ProgressBar>

     <ListBox Height="555" HorizontalAlignment="Left"
      Margin="2,6,0,0" Name="myEventsList"VerticalAlignment="Top"
      Width="448"></ListBox>

     <Button Content="Show Maps" Height="57"
      HorizontalAlignment="Left" Margin="294,549,0,0"
      Name="showMapButton" VerticalAlignment="Top" Width="156"
      FontSize="14" Click="showMap" />

     <my:Map Height="516"
      CredentialsProvider="xxxxxxxxxxxxxxx"
      HorizontalAlignment="Left" Margin="0,6,0,0" Name="myMap"
      VerticalAlignment="Top" Width="460" />
   </Grid>
   ```

4. In your `EventPage.xaml.cs` file, import the Maps namespace by adding the
   following line:

   ```
   using Microsoft.Phone.Controls.Maps;
   ```

5. Similarly, import the Location namespace by adding the following line in
   your `EventPage.xaml.cs` file:

   ```
   using System.Device.Location;
   ```

6. Your `EventPage.xaml` file should now look like the following screenshot:

7. Notice that we placed the maps and ListBox in the same grid and almost with same height; when we run the app at this stage now, the maps will be overlaid on top of the ListBox. However, we don't want that functionality; by default we will always show the ListBox (list of events) to the users, and when the user clicks on the **Show Maps** button, we will hide the ListBox and show the maps view and vice versa. To do this, we set the `Visible` property for the map control to `Collapsed` in the `EventPage()` constructor.

```
public EventPage()
{
  InitializeComponent();
  myMap.Visibility = Visibility.Collapsed;
  myEventsList.Visibility = Visibility.Visible;
  myWebClient = new WebClient();
}
```

8. The `showMapButton` is tied to the `showMap` method to handle the transition to/from the maps view to the ListBox view.

```
private void showMap(object sender, RoutedEventArgs e)
{
  if (myEventsList.Visibility == Visibility.Visible)
  {
    showMapButton.Content = "Switch to ListView";
    myMap.Visibility = Visibility.Visible;
    myMap.ZoomBarVisibility = Visibility.Visible;
    myEventsList.Visibility = Visibility.Collapsed;
  }
  else
    if (myMap.Visibility == Visibility.Visible)
    {
      showMapButton.Content = "Show Maps";
      myEventsList.Visibility = Visibility.Visible;
      myMap.Visibility = Visibility.Collapsed;
    }
}
```

9. To plot the events as **pushpins**, we need to use the latitude and longitude of each event from the `Eventful.com` API response XML. We do so by creating a new pushpin and assigning the latitude/longitude to the pushpin object, as well as the event name. Finally we add the pushpin to the map; this happens in a loop, depending upon the number of events retrieved from the `Eventful.com` API.

```
private void myWebClient_DownloadStringCompleted(object sender,
 DownloadStringCompletedEventArgs e)
{
  XElement xml = XElement.Parse(e.Result);
  loadingBar.IsIndeterminate = false;
  loadingBar.Visibility = Visibility.Collapsed;
  List<string>myListItem = newList<string>();
  IEnumerable<XElement> elements = xml.Descendants("event");

  String eventTitle, eventLatitude, eventLongitude;

  foreach (XElement element in elements)
  {
    Pushpin myPin = new Pushpin();
    eventTitle = element.Element("title").Value;
    myListItem.Add(eventTitle);
    eventLatitude = element.Element("latitude").Value;
```

```
          eventLongitude = element.Element("longitude").Value;

          myPin.Content = eventTitle;
          myPin.Background = new SolidColorBrush(Colors.Green);
          myPin.Location = new GeoCoordinate(
          Convert.ToDouble(eventLatitude),
          Convert.ToDouble(eventLongitude));
          myMap.Children.Add(myPin);
          myMap.SetView(newGeoCoordinate(
          Convert.ToDouble(eventLatitude),
          Convert.ToDouble(eventLongitude)), 14);
        }
      myEventsList.ItemsSource = myListItem;
    }
```

10. Running the application now produces the following results for the Events Page:

11. The **Show Maps** button changes to the Map Mode as shown in the following screenshot:

You can find this example project in the code files for the book under Chapter 4, titled HelloEvents-Maps.

Building the PacktEvents app using Panorama control

Pivot and **Panorama** are two visually appealing controls available in Windows Phone 7.5. If you have used the **Local Scout** app on your Nokia Lumia 800, you should have an idea of how the Panorama control works. We will use the Panorama control to build our PacktEvents application and in the next chapter we will use the Pivot control.

Visual Studio 2010 Express for Windows Phone has an option to select the **Windows Phone Panorama Application** template when choosing to create a **New Project**. However, we will not choose that path as the template comes with a lot of already built code and UI, whereas we want to learn to use the Panorama control from the ground up. So we start with the simple **Windows Phone Application** template and add the Panorama control by hand:

1. Fire up Visual Studio 2010 Express and create a **New Project** named `PacktEvents`, choosing the **Windows Phone Application** template.

2. From **Solution Explorer**, **Add Reference** to the `Microsoft.Phone.Controls` and `Microsoft.Phone.Controls.Maps` assemblies, as well as to the `System.Device` assembly.

3. Open `MainPage.xaml` and in the first XAML tag (`<phone:PhoneApplicationPage`), add the following code to import the Panorama and Pivot controls into your application:

   ```
   xmlns:controls="clr-
     namespace:Microsoft.Phone.Controls;assembly=
     Microsoft.Phone.Controls"
   ```

4. Delete everything between your `<Grid x:Name="LayoutRoot" Background="Transparent">` and `</Grid>` element and add the Panorama control as:

   ```
   <controls:Panorama Title="PacktEvents"
     Name="packtEventsPanorama">
   </controls:Panorama>
   ```

5. Add two Panorama items within your Panorama control by adding the following lines of code:

   ```
   <controls:PanoramaItem Header="Events"
    Name="eventsPanoramaItem">
   </controls:PanoramaItem>

   <controls:PanoramaItem Header="Venues"
    Name="venuesPanoramaItem">
   </controls:PanoramaItem>
   ```

6. Enable the Application Bar and enable just one Menu Item within it; we will use this to switch between the map and list views. Your full `MainPage.xaml` file should now look like the following screenshot:

7. We then add two `ListBox` control; one for Events and another for Venues. We also add a `TextBlock` control to notify the user of any application status messages.

```
<Grid x:Name="LayoutRoot" Background="Transparent">
  <TextBlock Height="30" HorizontalAlignment="Left"
    Margin="10,650,0,0" Name="statusText" Text="Status: "
    VerticalAlignment="Top" Width="444" />

    <controls:Panorama Title="PacktEvents"
      Name="packtEventsPanorama">
      <controls:PanoramaItem Header="Events"
        Name="eventsPanoramaItem">
        <ListBox Name="myEventList"></ListBox>
      </controls:PanoramaItem>

    <controls:PanoramaItem Header="Venues"
      Name="venuesPanoramaItem">
      <ListBox Name="myVenueList"></ListBox>
    </controls:PanoramaItem>
  </controls:Panorama>
</Grid>
```

8. In the Application Bar, we create a button that will refresh the content on demand.

```
<phone:PhoneApplicationPage.ApplicationBar>
  <shell:ApplicationBar IsVisible="True"
   IsMenuEnabled="True">
    <shell:ApplicationBarIconButton
     IconUri="/Images/appbar.sync.rest.png"
     Text="Refresh"/>
    <shell:ApplicationBar.MenuItems>
      <shell:ApplicationBarMenuItem Text="Show Maps"/>
    </shell:ApplicationBar.MenuItems>
  </shell:ApplicationBar>
</phone:PhoneApplicationPage.ApplicationBar>
```

9. The image has been sourced from our local installation of the Windows Phone 7.5 SDK - `C:\Program Files (x86)\Microsoft SDKs\Windows Phone\v7.1\Icons\light`.

10. We added an `Images` folder to our project and added the `appbar.sync.rest.png` file in it. Make sure you select the image and set the following properties:

    ° **Build Action: Content**
    ° **Copy to Output Directory: Copy if newer**

11. Speaking of images, we use a free icon for the app icon – courtesy of `WebIconSet.com` – and replace the default `ApplicationIcon.png` with the new one. The following screenshot shows how our application icon looks on the device:

12. For our main Panorama control, we define a `SelectionChanged` event handler that will be used to identify whether the Events or the Venues Panorama item is being displayed on the screen at any given point of time. Based on this, we will call the respective `Eventful.com` API.

```
<controls:Panorama Title="PacktEvents"
 Name="packtEventsPanorama"SelectionChanged="changeData">
```

13. The following lines of code shows how we find the selected Panorama item and call the appropriate API via multiple `WebClient` objects:

```
private void changeData(object sender, EventArgs e)
{
  if(packtEventsPanorama.SelectedIndex==0)
  {
  // Load Events from Eventful.com API
    loadingBar.IsVisible = true;
    Uri uri = new Uri
    ("http://api.eventful.com/rest/events/search?location=" +
    latitude + "," + longitude + "&app_key=" + apiKey +
    "&within=10");

    if (!myEventsWebClient.IsBusy)
    {
        myEventsWebClient.DownloadStringAsync(uri);
    }
      // End of Eventful API call.
  }

  if (packtEventsPanorama.SelectedIndex == 1)
  {
    // Load Venues from Eventful.com API
    loadingBar.IsVisible = true;
    Uri uri = new Uri
     ("http://api.eventful.com/rest/venues/search?location=" +
     latitude + "," + longitude + "&app_key=" + apiKey +
     "&within=10");

    if (!myVenuesWebClient.IsBusy)
      {
        myVenuesWebClient.DownloadStringAsync(uri);
      }
      // End of Eventful API call.
  }
}
```

14. We defined the multiple `WebClient` objects in our `MainPage()` constructor; we also declare separate callback functions:

```
myEventsWebClient = new WebClient();
myVenuesWebClient = new WebClient();

myEventsWebClient.DownloadStringCompleted += new
 DownloadStringCompletedEventHandler
```

```
(myEvents_DownloadStringCompleted);

myVenuesWebClient.DownloadStringCompleted += new
 DownloadStringCompletedEventHandler
 (myVenues_DownloadStringCompleted);
```

15. To show a loading bar every time our application hits the `Eventful.com` API, we add a shell tray within our Application Bar in the `MainPage.xaml` file.

```
<shell:SystemTray.ProgressIndicator>
  <shell:ProgressIndicator IsIndeterminate="True"
   IsVisible="True" Text="Loading ..."
   x:Name="loadingBar" />
</shell:SystemTray.ProgressIndicator>
```

16. The rest of the code is quite similar to our previous example, however, if you run into trouble, you can find this example project in the code files for the book under `Chapter 4`, titled `PacktEvents`.

17. Running the application in the emulator produces the following result:

18. Move over to the **Venues** Panorama item, you should see the nearby venues around your detected location as shown in the following screenshot:

19. Note, we start and stop the Location Services using the OnNavigatedTo and OnNavigatedFrom overridable methods of the PhoneApplicationPage class.

```
protected override void
 OnNavigatedTo(System.Windows.Navigation.NavigationEventArgs e)
{
  base.OnNavigatedTo(e);
  locationManager.Start();
}

protected override void
 OnNavigatedFrom
 (System.Windows.Navigation.NavigationEventArgse)
{
  base.OnNavigatedFrom(e);
  locationManager.Stop();
}
```

Feel free to add more customizations, pages, icons, and code in the application. Send it across to me via the book's forum page at `http://books.justgeeks.in`, and I will be glad to incorporate new code, comments in the application, and maybe even publish this app on the Windows Phone Marketplace! You can also contact me on Twitter, `@imzeeshan` for any questions you may have about the book, and I will do my best to address it.

Summary

In this chapter we learnt how to build our first location-based app for Windows Phone 7.5 using the awesome `Eventful.com` API.

Specifically, we covered the `Eventful.com` API and using this, extended the `Hello Location` example by showing nearby events. We also looked at filtering events by categories and plotting events on Bing Maps. Lastly, we learnt to build the `PacktEvents` app using the Panorama control.

In the next chapter we will create another Windows Phone Application that uses AOL's `Patch.com` News API to build a location-aware news app. So keep reading.

5
Location-aware News App – PacktNews

Hyperlocal applications and websites such as AOL's `Patch.com` provide precise and accurate news up to the neighborhood level, based on the user's location. In this chapter, we will learn to build a location-aware news application for Windows Phone 7.5 – titled `PacktNews` – using AOL's Patch News API.

This chapter covers:

- Understanding the Patch News API
- Consuming the Patch News API – `HelloNews`
- Building the `PacktNews` app using the Silverlight for Windows Phone 7.5 Pivot control

Understanding the Patch News API

AOL's `Patch.com` is a hyperlocal news portal that provides comprehensive and trusted local content to its users, and is powered by editors, writers, photographers, and videographers who live nearby.

Patch has a huge editorial team as well as freelance bloggers that help create original content, and which is published to a network of more than 850 sites. Patch local content includes news, events, business listings, photos, videos, and announcements. The geotagged hyperlocal content is available for third-party consumption via the Developer API at `http://developers.patch.com/`, which we will use to build our `PacktNews` app.

Before we move further towards building our app, lets us have a good look at the API calls provided by `Patch.com` and their structure. The Patch News API has the following four main components:

- Authentication
- Taxonomy (Categories)
- Finding stories by location
- Finding locations by name

Authentication

Any app or website that intends to use the Patch News API must obtain authentication. The authentication is a combination of your **developer key**, **secret key** and the current **timestamp**, all combined together and converted to a **MD5** hash key. Unfortunately, the core platform for Windows Phone 7.5 does not support MD5 yet; however, there is a Silverlight MD5 implementation available from MSDN at `http://archive.msdn.microsoft.com/SilverlightMD5` that we will use to perform the authentication for the Patch News API. The following is a snippet of code to get the MD5 hash via the `MD5Managed` class within a simple Windows Phone app:

```
public MainPage()
{
  InitializeComponent();

  string key = "xxxxxxxx";// Get key and secret from
  //http://developers.patch.com/
  string secret = "xxxxxxx";
  inttimeInSecs = (int)(DateTime.UtcNow -newDateTime(1970,
    1, 1)).TotalSeconds;

  MD5Managed md5 = newMD5Managed();
  byte[] bs = System.Text.Encoding.UTF8.GetBytes(key + secret
    + timeInSecs);
  byte[] hash = md5.ComputeHash(bs);


  StringBuildersb = newStringBuilder();
  foreach (byte b in hash)
  {
    sb.Append(b.ToString("x2").ToLower());
  }

  stringurl = "http://news-api.patch.com/v1.1/nearby/
```

```
    37.785368,-122.441654/stories?dev_key=" + key +
    "&sig=" + sb;

  Debug.WriteLine(url);
}
```

Taxonomy

Patch organizes news stories into three main taxonomy types:

- **Vertical**: Topic of the content
- **Format**: Medium from which the content was found
- **Author type**: Who wrote the content—an individual or a business

These taxonomies are further classified as:

- Vertical:
  - News
  - Lifestyle
  - Education
  - Business
  - Science and technology
  - Sports

- Format:
  - Stories
  - Reviews and ratings
  - Event listings

- Author type:
  - Individuals
  - Businesses and organizations
  - Educational institutions
  - Government
  - Sharing and community sites
  - Independent news media
  - Mainstream media such as CNN and NY Times

Finding stories by location

The Patch News API supports location-based search for stories, by using any of the following parameters:

- State
- City
- Zip code
- Neighborhood
- Nearby
- Patch location **universally unique identifier** (**UUID**) (`Patch.com` internal city/state and neighborhood IDs), which can be retrieved by the *find locations by name* method described in the next section

Finding locations by name

Patch News API supports a location retrieval API call that accepts a text string and returns well-formatted location information, something similar to the GeoNames API and/or reverse geocoding.

The result of the query includes the UUID as discussed in the previous segment; this is useful if you are building an offline application, for example, an application for San Francisco city that uses the San Francisco UUID hardcoded in the application. Another use case would be to store content offline tagged with the UUID.

Locations to be queried could be any of the following parameters:

- States
- Cities
- Zip codes
- Neighborhoods
- Places
- Localities
- Metro areas

Full documentation can be found at `http://developers.patch.com/docs/`.

Consuming the Patch News API – HelloNews

Having had a detailed look at the Patch News API, let us fire some code to consume it:

1. Start Visual Studio 2010 Express and create a new **Windows Phone Application** named `HelloNews`.

2. Download the `MD5Managed` class from `http://archive.msdn.microsoft.com/SilverlightMD5`, and add it your solution using the Solution Explorer's **Add | Existing Item** option.

3. Download the `Json.NET` library from `codeplex.com` at `http://json.codeplex.com/`; extracting it creates the `Json45r7\Bin\WindowsPhone` directory which contains the files we need. We will use this library to parse JSON within our example application.

4. Add the `Json.NET` library to your solution as a reference by browsing to the directory where you have downloaded the library; see the following screenshot:

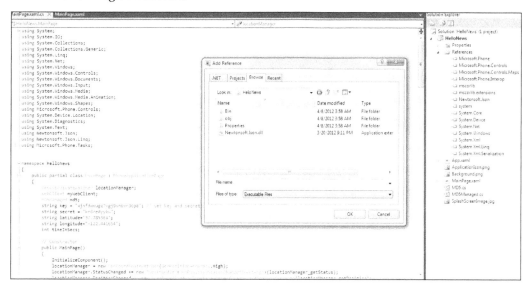

5. Import `System.Device.Location`, `System.Text`, `System.Diagnostics`, `Microsoft.Phone.Tasks`, `Newtonsoft.Json`, and the `Newtonsoft.Json.Linq` namespaces as shown in the following code snippet within your `MainPage.xaml.cs` file:

```
Using System.Device.Location;
Using System.Diagnostics;
Using System.Text;
```

```
Using Newtonsoft.Json;
Using Newtonsoft.Json.Linq;
Using Microsoft.Phone.Tasks;
```

6. Our UI will be simple; just a `ListBox` control for showing the **Nearby Stories** (news), a `ProgressBar` control for a good user experience, and a `TextBlock` control for displaying the location status, as shown in the following screenshot:

7. The following code snippet implements the screenshot shown in the previous step:

```xml
<Grid x:Name="ContentPanel" Grid.Row="1" Margin="12,0,12,0">
  <ListBox Height="569" HorizontalAlignment="Left"
   Name="myStoryBox" VerticalAlignment="Top"
   Width="456" Tap="fireWeb" />
  <ProgressBar Name="loadingBar"
   IsIndeterminate="True"></ProgressBar>
  <TextBlock Height="30"HorizontalAlignment="Left"
   Margin="10,575,0,0" Name="statusText"
   Text="Status: "VerticalAlignment="Top"
   Width="444" />
</Grid>
```

8. Within our `MainPage` class define the location manager, web client, timestamp, key, and secret for the Patch News API, as well as the `latitude` and `longitude` variables, and the `MD5Managed` object as follows:

```
GeoCoordinateWatcher locationManager;
WebClient myWebClient;
MD5Managed md5;
string key = "xxxxx"; // Get key and secret from
// http://developers.patch.com/
string secret = " xxxxx ";
string latitude="37.785368";
string longitude="-122.441654";
int timeInSecs;
```

9. Now within the `MainPage()` constructor, initialize the variables needed for generating the MD5 hash:

```
public MainPage()
{
  InitializeComponent();
  locationManager = new GeoCoordinateWatcher
   (GeoPositionAccuracy.High);
  locationManager.StatusChanged += new
   EventHandler<GeoPositionStatusChangedEventArgs>
   (locationManager_getStatus);

  locationManager.PositionChanged += new
   EventHandler<GeoPositionChangedEventArgs<GeoCoordinate>>
   (locationManager_getPosition);

  myWebClient = new WebClient();
  md5 = newMD5Managed();

  timeInSecs = (int)(DateTime.UtcNow - newDateTime(1970, 1,
   1)).TotalSeconds;
}
```

10. The `locationManager_getStatus` method remains the same as from our previous examples in the code; we just check the status of the `locationManager` object based on `GeoPositionStatus`, and notify the user via `TextBlock` near the footer of the application.

11. However, the `locationManager_getPosition` method is updated to include a timestamp-based MD5 hash in the authentication URL for the Patch News API, as well as to fetch the nearby stories from the API.

```
void locationManager_getPosition(object sender,
 GeoPositionChangedEventArgs<GeoCoordinate>newLoc)
{
```

```
myStoryBox.Items.Clear();

latitude = newLoc.Position.Location.Latitude.ToString();
longitude = newLoc.Position.Location.Longitude.ToString();

loadingBar.IsIndeterminate = true;
loadingBar.Visibility = Visibility.Visible;

// Start MD5 process
byte[] bs = System.Text.Encoding.UTF8.GetBytes
  (key + secret + timeInSecs);
byte[] hash = md5.ComputeHash(bs);

StringBuilder sb = new StringBuilder();

foreach (byte b in hash)
{
    sb.Append(b.ToString("x2").ToLower());
}
// End of MD5 process

string url = "http://news-api.patch.com/v1.1/nearby/" +
  latitude + ","+longitude +"/stories?dev_key=" +
  key + "&sig=" + sb+"&radius=5000";

myWebClient.DownloadStringCompleted +=
  new DownloadStringCompletedEventHandler
  (myWebClient_DownloadStringCompleted);

Uri uri = new Uri(url);

if (!myWebClient.IsBusy)
{
    myWebClient.DownloadStringAsync(uri);
    Debug.WriteLine(url);
}

}
```

12. The `StringBuilder` class is declared in the `System.Text` namespace; hence we imported it in step 5.

13. The `locationManager` object is started within the `OnNavigatedTo` method as shown in the following code:

```
protected override void
  OnNavigatedTo(System.Windows.Navigation.NavigationEventArgs e)
{
```

```
   base.OnNavigatedTo(e);
   locationManager.Start();
}
```

14. When the web client's request is complete and the callback method is called, we use the `Json.NET` library to parse the JSON payload, and pass it to our UI for display via the `ListBox` control:

```
private void myWebClient_DownloadStringCompleted(object sender,
 DownloadStringCompletedEventArgs e)
{

  JObject json=
    (JObject)JsonConvert.DeserializeObject(e.Result);

  int i = 1;

  foreach (var story in json["stories"])
  {
    String titleText = (string) story["title"];
    String storyUrl = (string)story["story_url"];

    StackPanel storyStackPanel = new StackPanel();
    storyStackPanel.Name = storyUrl;

    TextBlock titleTextBlock = new TextBlock();
    titleTextBlock.TextWrapping = TextWrapping.Wrap;
    titleTextBlock.Name = "titleTextBlock" + titleText;
    titleTextBlock.Text = i + ") " +titleText + ".\n";
    titleTextBlock.FontSize = 28;

    storyStackPanel.Children.Add(titleTextBlock);
    myStoryBox.Items.Add(storyStackPanel);
    i++;
  }

  loadingBar.IsIndeterminate = false;
  loadingBar.Visibility = Visibility.Collapsed;
}
```

15. Notice the highlighted code in the previous step: we use the `JObject` class from the `Json.NET` library to convert the JSON data into a `JObject` instance named `json`. We parse each story and prepend an integer value to each story title. We add a **stack panel** and within the stack panel, a `TextBlock` control holding the story title. We then add the `StackPanel` object to the `ListBox` control for display.

16. Notice how we use the `story_url` data from JSON; we use it on the `Tap` event (method name `fireWeb`) of the `ListBox` control, and use the `WebBrowserTask` launcher to launch the URL specified by the `story_url` field:

```
private void fireWeb(object sender, GestureEventArgs e)
{
  StackPanel selectedStory = new StackPanel();
  selectedStory = myStoryBox.SelectedItem as StackPanel;
  WebBrowserTask web = new WebBrowserTask();
  web.Uri = new Uri(selectedStory.Name);
  web.Show();
}
```

17. Running the project in the emulator produces the following result:

18. Clicking on any news item will open the browser with the appropriate news URL, as shown in the following screenshot:

You can find this example project in the code files for the book under `Chapter 5`, titled `HelloNews`.

Building the PacktNews app using the Silverlight for Windows Phone 7.5 Pivot control

Now that we have learnt how to use the Patch News API, let us move ahead to build our `PacktNews` app using the Windows Phone Pivot control. We will use a free icon from `http://findicons.com/icon/169293/news?id=376465#` for the `PacktNews` app.

It is also a good idea to have a look at the taxonomy (in other words, category structure) of the Patch News API. There are two levels of taxonomy supported: category and subcategory level, as shown in the following table:

Taxonomy type	Category	Subcategory
Vertical	news	national
		local
		crime
		politics-and-political-analysis
		opinion
	lifestyle	activism
		arts-and-entertainment
		crafts
		fashion
		food-and-restaurants
		nightlife
		shopping
		real-estate
		health
		travel
		recreation
		parenting-family-and-children
		personal
		religion
		community
	education	colleges-and-universities
		high-schools
		libraries
	business	finance
		marketing
		small-business
		advertising
		business-promotion
	science-and-technology	
	sports	

Taxonomy type	Category	Subcategory
Format	stories	blog-posts
		news-articles
		press-releases
	reviews-and-ratings	
	event-listings	
Author type	mainstream-media	
	independent-new-media	
	sharing-and-community-sites	
	business-and-organizations	corporations
		small-businesses
		real-estate-agents-and-brokers
		non-profit-and-not-for-profit-organizations
		sports-teams
		religious-institutions
		political-parties
	individuals	general
		celebrities
	educational-institutions	colleges-and-universities
		high-schools
		libraries
	government	

These taxonomies can be used with include or exclude parameters, based on the taxonomy type. For example, the `&author-type=individuals` parameter can be used to fetch news stories submitted by individuals only. We will use a combination of these taxonomies to build `PacktNews`, so let's get started:

1. Create a new **Windows Phone Application** from Visual Studio 2010 Express and name it `PacktNews`.

2. We will need the `MD5Managed.cs` file from the previous example, so include that in your project. Add the `Json.NET` (`Newtonsoft.Json`) to your project by adding a reference to the downloaded DLL file. It is a good idea to copy the DLL and any other referenced files within your project folder.

3. As we will be using the Pivot control, we need to add the `Windows.Phone.Controls` namespace to our `MainPage.xaml` by adding the following code within the `<phone:PhoneApplicationPage>` tag:

```
xmlns:controls="clr-namespace:
  Microsoft.Phone.Controls;assembly=Microsoft.Phone.Controls"
```

4. Add a Pivot control to the `Grid` named `ContentPanel`, and name it `"packtNewsPivot"`.

```
<controls:Pivot Title="PactkNews" Name="packtNewsPivot"
  SelectionChanged="changeData">
```

5. The `changeData` method is called on the `SelectionChanged` event; this triggers when we switch between the multiple pivot items.

6. We add three `PivotItem` controls to the parent pivot: one for `News`, another for showing nearby `Places`, and the third one for nearby `Events`. Each pivot item has its own `ListBox`: `myNewsBox`, `myPlacesBox`, and `myEventsBox` respectively.

7. We add an **Application Bar** and **system shell tray** with a **progress indicator**, similarly to how we did in the `PacktEvents` app in *Chapter 4, Events App - PacktEvents*.

8. The full source code of the `MainPage.xaml` file is shown as follows:

```
<phone:PhoneApplicationPage
  x:Class="PacktNews.MainPage"
  xmlns="http://schemas.microsoft.com/winfx/2006/
    xaml/presentation"
  xmlns:x="http://schemas.microsoft.com/winfx/2006/xaml"
  xmlns:phone="clr-namespace:
    Microsoft.Phone.Controls;assembly=Microsoft.Phone"
  xmlns:shell="clr-namespace:
    Microsoft.Phone.Shell;assembly=Microsoft.Phone"
  xmlns:controls="clr-namespace:
    Microsoft.Phone.Controls;assembly=Microsoft.Phone.Controls"

  xmlns:d="http://schemas.microsoft.com/expression/blend/2008"
  xmlns:mc="http://schemas.openxmlformats.org/markup-
    compatibility/2006"
  mc:Ignorable="d" d:DesignWidth="480" d:DesignHeight="696"
  FontFamily="{StaticResourcePhoneFontFamilyNormal}"
  FontSize="{StaticResourcePhoneFontSizeNormal}"
  Foreground="{StaticResourcePhoneForegroundBrush}"
  SupportedOrientations="Portrait" Orientation="Portrait"
  shell:SystemTray.IsVisible="True">
```

```xml
<!--LayoutRoot is the root grid where all page content is
 placed-->
  <Grid x:Name="LayoutRoot" Background="Transparent">

  <!--ContentPanel - place additional content here-->
    <Grid x:Name="ContentPanel" Grid.Row="1"
      Margin="12,0,12,0">
        <TextBlock Height="30"HorizontalAlignment="Left"
          Margin="20,130,0,0" Name="statusText"
          Text="Status: "VerticalAlignment="Top"
          Width="444" />

        <controls:Pivot Title="PactkNews"
          Name="packtNewsPivot"
          SelectionChanged="changeData">
            <controls:PivotItem Header="News">
              <ListBox Height="569"
                HorizontalAlignment="Left"
                Name="myNewsBox"
                VerticalAlignment="Top"
                Width="456" Tap="fireWeb" />
            </controls:PivotItem>

            <controls:PivotItem Header="Places">
              <ListBox Height="569"
                HorizontalAlignment="Left"
                Name="myPlacesBox"
                VerticalAlignment="Top"
                Width="456" Tap="fireWeb" />
            </controls:PivotItem>

            <controls:PivotItem Header="Events">
              <ListBox Height="569"
                HorizontalAlignment="Left"
                Name="myEventsBox"
                VerticalAlignment="Top"
                Width="456" Tap="fireWeb" />
            </controls:PivotItem>
          </controls:Pivot>

      </Grid>
    </Grid>

<phone:PhoneApplicationPage.ApplicationBar>
    <shell:ApplicationBarIsVisible="True"
      IsMenuEnabled="True">
```

```xml
      <shell:ApplicationBarIconButton
       IconUri="/Images/appbar.sync.rest.png"
       Click="changeData" Text="Refresh"/>
      <shell:ApplicationBar.MenuItems>
        <shell:ApplicationBarMenuItem Text="Settings"/>
      </shell:ApplicationBar.MenuItems>
    </shell:ApplicationBar>
  </phone:PhoneApplicationPage.ApplicationBar>

  <shell:SystemTray.ProgressIndicator>
    <shell:ProgressIndicatorIsIndeterminate="True"
     IsVisible="True" Text="Loading ..."
     x:Name="loadingBar" />
  </shell:SystemTray.ProgressIndicator>

</phone:PhoneApplicationPage>
```

9. Notice that we added a Refresh menu button in the Application Bar, which calls the `changeData` method to reload the content from the API—on demand.

10. Most of our code in the `MainPage.xaml.cs` file will be similar to the `HelloNews` example we saw earlier. However, some new variables and methods are introduced in the `PacktNews` project to handle each of the three pivot items.

11. We begin by declaring three instances of `WebClient` in our main class:

```
WebClient myNewsWebclient,
myPlacesWebClient,myEventsWebClient;
```

12. The three instances of `WebClient` mentioned in the previous step have their own callback functions defined in the `MainPage()` constructor:

```
myNewsWebclient = new WebClient();
myPlacesWebClient = new WebClient();
myEventsWebClient = new WebClient();

myNewsWebclient.DownloadStringCompleted += new
 DownloadStringCompletedEventHandler
 (myNewsWebclient_DownloadStringCompleted);
myPlacesWebClient.DownloadStringCompleted += new
 DownloadStringCompletedEventHandler
 (myPlacesWebClient_DownloadStringCompleted);
myEventsWebClient.DownloadStringCompleted += new
 DownloadStringCompletedEventHandler
 (myEventsWebClientDownloadStringCompleted);
```

13. The `changeData` method detects which pivot item has been selected, and makes the appropriate API call to the Patch News API. For the `News` pivot, we use the general API we saw in the `HelloNews` example. However, for the `Places` pivot, we call the API with some additional parameters by examining the Patch News API closely. These parameters return us stories for specific **verticals**, in our case we will choose `lifestyle | food-and-restaurants`, `lifestyle | arts-and-entertainment`, and `lifestyle | nightlife` verticals. Similarly, for the `Events` pivot, we will use the `format=event-listings` parameter in the API call:

```
private void changeData(object sender, EventArgs e)
{
  // Start MD5 process
  byte[] bs = System.Text.Encoding.UTF8.GetBytes(key + secret
    + timeInSecs);
  byte[] hash = md5.ComputeHash(bs);

  StringBuilder sb = new StringBuilder();
  foreach (byte b in hash)
  {
    sb.Append(b.ToString("x2").ToLower());
  }
  // End of MD5 process

  if (packtNewsPivot.SelectedIndex == 0)
  {
    loadingBar.IsVisible = true;
    Uri uri = new Uri("http://news-api.patch.com/v1.1/nearby/"
      + latitude + "," + longitude + "/stories?dev_key=" + key +
      "&sig=" + sb + "&radius=5000");

    if (!myNewsWebclient.IsBusy)
    {
      myNewsWebclient.DownloadStringAsync(uri);
    }
  }
  else
  if (packtNewsPivot.SelectedIndex == 1)
  {
    loadingBar.IsVisible = true;
    Uri uri = new Uri("http://news.api.patch.com/v1.1/nearby/
      "+ latitude + "," + longitude + "/stories?dev_key=" + key
      + "&sig=" + sb + "&radius=5000&vertical=lifestyle
      &vertical=food-and-restaurants&vertical=arts-and-
      entertainment&vertical=nightlife");
```

```
      if (!myPlacesWebClient.IsBusy)
      {
        myPlacesWebClient.DownloadStringAsync(uri);
      }
    }
    else
      if (packtNewsPivot.SelectedIndex == 2)
      {
        loadingBar.IsVisible = true;
        Uri uri = newUri("http://news-
        api.patch.com/v1.1/nearby/" + latitude +
         "," + longitude + "/stories?dev_key=" + key + "&sig="
         + sb + "&radius=5000&format=event-listings");

        if (!myEventsWebClient.IsBusy)
        {
          myEventsWebClient.DownloadStringAsync(uri);
        }
      }
  }
```

14. The `myNewsWebclient_DownloadStringCompleted`, `myPlacesWebClient_DownloadStringCompleted`, and `myEventsWebClientDownloadStringCompleted` methods are quite similar, except for the distinction that they fill their respective list boxes with the data parsed from the JSON payload, received from the respective API calls. For the sake of clarity, the `myNewsWebclient_DownloadStringCompleted` method is shown as follows:

```
private void myNewsWebclient_DownloadStringCompleted(object
  sender, DownloadStringCompletedEventArgs e)
{
  myNewsBox.Items.Clear();

  JObject
    json=(JObject)JsonConvert.DeserializeObject(e.Result);
  int i = 1;

  foreach (var story in json["stories"])
    {
      String titleText = (string)story["title"];
      String storyUrl = (string)story["story_url"];

      StackPanel storyStackPanel = new StackPanel();
      storyStackPanel.Name = storyUrl;
```

```
    TextBlock titleTextBlock = new TextBlock();
    titleTextBlock.TextWrapping = TextWrapping.Wrap;
    titleTextBlock.Name = "titleTextBlock" + titleText;
    titleTextBlock.Text = i + ") " +titleText + ".\n";
    titleTextBlock.FontSize = 28;

    storyStackPanel.Children.Add(titleTextBlock);
    myNewsBox.Items.Add(storyStackPanel);
    i++;
  }
  loadingBar.IsVisible = false;
}
```

15. Running the application in the emulator produces the following screenshot (with location as New York):

16. The Places pivot page looks like the following screenshot:

17. And finally, the Events pivot page looks like the following screenshot:

18. Remember from the XAML code, we added the `Tap="fireWeb"` code to each of the three list boxes. The `fireWeb` method detects which pivot item is selected and gets the selected `StackPanel` object and the `Name` attribute. (We use the `Name` attribute of the `StackPanel` object to pass the story URL to the `WebBrowserTask`.)

```
private void fireWeb(object sender, GestureEventArgs e)
{
  StackPanel selectedStory = new StackPanel();
  WebBrowserTask web = new WebBrowserTask();

  if (packtNewsPivot.SelectedIndex == 0)
  {
    selectedStory = myNewsBox.SelectedItemasStackPanel;
  }
  else
    if (packtNewsPivot.SelectedIndex == 1)
    {
      selectedStory = myPlacesBox.SelectedItemasStackPanel;
    }
    else
    {
      selectedStory = myEventsBox.SelectedItemasStackPanel;
    }

  web.Uri = new Uri(selectedStory.Name);
  web.Show();
}
```

19. Clicking on any news story from any of the pivot items would fire up the web browser on your Windows Phone and launch the news story page, as shown in the following screenshot:

You can find this example project in the code files for the book under `Chapter 5`, titled `PacktNews`.

Summary

In this concluding chapter, we learnt how to build a location-aware news app for Windows Phone 7.5 using the Pivot control and AOL's Patch News API.

Specifically, we covered understanding the Patch News API and consuming it to build our `PacktNews` app using the Pivot control.

This book is not the end of our learning. I will be maintaining a forum for this book at `http://books.justgeeks.in`, where I will be updating the source code for the applications discussed in this book, as well as discussions, suggestions, and errata.

Index

U

universally unique identifier. *See* UUID
UUID 110

V

Visioglobe 19
Visual Studio 2010 Express 28

W

Wi-Fi based location detection
  about 14
  Skyhook Wireless, working 14, 15
Windows Phone 7.5
  about 7, 21
  developer tools 25
  key functionality 23
  LBS, using 10
  maps, using 50-57
Windows Phone 7.5 Pivot control
  Patch News API building, Silverlight used
    117-128

Windows Phone Bing Maps Silverlight
    Control
  overview 50
Windows Phone Location Service
  about 29-31
  accuracy levels 36
  monitoring 36-41
  simulator, working with 42-44
  starting 32-36
  using 32-36
Windows Phone Marketplace 22

X

XAML 29
XElement.Parse method 68

Z

Zune music player 79

Thank you for buying
Windows Phone 7.5: Building Location-aware Applications

About Packt Publishing

Packt, pronounced 'packed', published its first book "Mastering phpMyAdmin for Effective MySQL Management" in April 2004 and subsequently continued to specialize in publishing highly focused books on specific technologies and solutions.

Our books and publications share the experiences of your fellow IT professionals in adapting and customizing today's systems, applications, and frameworks. Our solution based books give you the knowledge and power to customize the software and technologies you're using to get the job done. Packt books are more specific and less general than the IT books you have seen in the past. Our unique business model allows us to bring you more focused information, giving you more of what you need to know, and less of what you don't.

Packt is a modern, yet unique publishing company, which focuses on producing quality, cutting-edge books for communities of developers, administrators, and newbies alike. For more information, please visit our website: www.packtpub.com.

About Packt Enterprise

In 2010, Packt launched two new brands, Packt Enterprise and Packt Open Source, in order to continue its focus on specialization. This book is part of the Packt Enterprise brand, home to books published on enterprise software – software created by major vendors, including (but not limited to) IBM, Microsoft and Oracle, often for use in other corporations. Its titles will offer information relevant to a range of users of this software, including administrators, developers, architects, and end users.

Writing for Packt

We welcome all inquiries from people who are interested in authoring. Book proposals should be sent to author@packtpub.com. If your book idea is still at an early stage and you would like to discuss it first before writing a formal book proposal, contact us; one of our commissioning editors will get in touch with you.

We're not just looking for published authors; if you have strong technical skills but no writing experience, our experienced editors can help you develop a writing career, or simply get some additional reward for your expertise.

Windows Phone 7 Silverlight Cookbook

ISBN: 978-1-84969-116-1   Paperback: 304 pages

All the recipes you need to start creating apps and making money

1. Build sophisticated Windows Phone apps with clean, optimized code.

2. Perform easy to follow recipes to create practical apps.

3. Master the entire workflow from designing your app to publishing it.

Windows Phone 7.5 Data Cookbook

ISBN: 978-1-84969-122-2   Paperback: 224 pages

Over 30 recipes for storing, managing, and manipulating data in Windows Phone 7.5 Mango applications

1. Simple data binding recipes to advanced recipes for building scalable applications.

2. Techniques for managing application data in Windows Phone mango apps.

3. On-device data storage, cloud storage and API interaction.

Please check **www.PacktPub.com** for information on our titles

Windows Phone 7 XNA Cookbook

ISBN: 978-1-84969-120-8   Paperback: 450 pages

Over 70 recipes for making your own Windows Phone 7 game

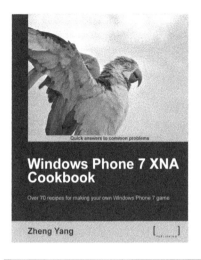

1. Complete focus on the best Windows Phone 7 game development techniques using XNA 4.0.

2. Easy to follow cookbook allowing you to dive in wherever you want.

3. Convert ideas into action using practical recipes.

Microsoft SharePoint 2010 Enterprise Applications on Windows Phone 7

ISBN: 978-1-84968-258-9   Paperback: 252 pages

Create enterprise-ready websites and applications that access Microsoft SharePoint on Windows Phone 7

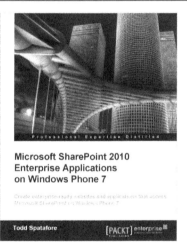

1. Provides step-by-step instructions for integrating Windows Phone 7-capable web pages into SharePoint websites.

2. Provides an overview of creating Windows Phone 7 applications that integrate with SharePoint services.

3. Examines Windows Phone 7's enterprise capabilities.

Please check **www.PacktPub.com** for information on our titles

www.ingramcontent.com/pod-product-compliance
Lightning Source LLC
LaVergne TN
LVHW080059070326
832902LV00014B/2308